Editorial Project Manager
Lorin E. Klistoff, M.A.

Managing Editor
Ina Massler Levin, M.A.

Illustrator
Alexandra Artigas

Cover Artist
Barb Lorseyedi

Creative Director
Karen J. Goldfluss, M.S. Ed.

Art Production Manager
Kevin Barnes

Art Coordinator
Renée Christine Yates

Imaging
James Edward Grace

Publisher
Mary D. Smith, M.S. Ed.

Full-Color STANDARDS-BASED MATH Activities & Games

Includes Standards & Benchmarks

Authors

Judy Kvaale, M.S., Sue Lundgren, M.S., and Jennifer Von Pinnon, M.S.

The classroom teacher may reproduce copies of materials in this book for classroom use only. Reproduction of any part for an entire school or school system is strictly prohibited. No part of this publication may be transmitted, stored, or recorded in any form without written permission from the publisher.

Teacher Created Resources, Inc.
6421 Industry Way
Westminster, CA 92683
www.teachercreated.com
ISBN-13: 978-1-4206-8719-4

©2007 Teacher Created Resources, Inc.
Made in U.S.A.

Table of Contents

Introduction 4

Addition (Addition Bowling) 5
  Standard: Uses basic and advanced procedures while performing the processes of computation
  Benchmark: Performs basic mental computations

Algebra (Big Money Math) 13
  Standard: Understands and applies basic and advanced properties of functions and algebra
  Benchmark: Knows that a variable is a letter or symbol that stands for one or more numbers
  Benchmark: Understands the basic concept of an equality relationship (i.e., an equation is a number sentence that shows two quantities that are equal)
  Benchmark: Solves simple open sentences involving operations on whole numbers (e.g., ? + 17 = 23)

Decimals (Get to the Point) 27
  Standard: Understands and applies basic and advanced properties of the concepts of numbers
  Benchmark: Understands the relative magnitude and relationships among whole numbers, fractions, decimals, and mixed numbers

Decimals, Fractions, and Mixed Numbers (Place Your Order) 35
  Standard: Understands and applies basic and advanced properties of the concepts of numbers
  Benchmark: Understands the relative magnitude and relationships among whole numbers, fractions, decimals, and mixed numbers

Division (M.A.T.H.) 43
  Standard: Understands and applies basic and advanced properties of the concepts of numbers
  Benchmark: Understands basic number theory concepts

Elapsed Time (Time Flies) 53
  Standard: Understands and applies basic and advanced properties of the concepts of measurement
  Benchmark: Understands relationships between measures

Fractions (Pizza Delivery) 61
  Standard: Understands and applies basic and advanced properties of the concepts of numbers
  Benchmark: Understands the relative magnitude and relationships among whole numbers, fractions, decimals, and mixed numbers

Geometry: Area and Perimeter (Inside and Out) 81
  Standard: Understands and applies basic and advanced properties of the concepts of measurement
  Benchmark: Understands the basic measures of perimeter, area, volume, capacity, mass, angle, and circumference

Measurement: Capacity (Fill 'Er Up) 89
  Standard: Understands and applies basic and advanced properties of the concepts of measurement
  Benchmark: Understands the basic measures of perimeter, area, volume, capacity, mass, angle, and circumference

*All standards listed above are from *A Compendium of Standards and Benchmarks for K–12 Education* (Copyright 2004 McREL, www.mcrel.org/standards-benchmarks) Mathematics (Grades 3–5).

Table of Contents

Measurement: Weight (Ounce or Pound?) 101
   Standard: Understands and applies basic and advanced properties of the concepts of measurement
   Benchmark: Understands relationships between measures

Number Patterns (Powerful Patterns) 103
   Standard: Understands and applies basic and advanced properties of functions and algebra
   Benchmark: Recognizes a wide variety of patterns and the rules that explain them

Place Value (Place Value Victory) 111
   Standard: Understands and applies basic and advanced properties of the concepts of numbers
   Benchmark: Understands the basic meaning of place value

Probability (Take a Chance) 123
   Standard: Understands and applies basic and advanced concepts of probability
   Benchmark: Recognizes events that are sure to happen, events that are sure not to happen, and events that may or may not happen (e.g., in terms of "certain," "likely," and "unlikely")

Problem Solving (Problem Solving Speedway) 131
   Standard: Uses a variety of strategies in the problem-solving process
   Benchmark: Uses a variety of strategies to understand problem situations

Subtraction: No Regrouping and Regrouping (Subtraction Bowling) 145
   Standard: Uses basic and advanced procedures while performing the processes of computation
   Benchmark: Performs basic mental computations

Vocabulary: Math Terms (The Terminator) 157
   Standard: Uses basic and advanced procedures while performing the processes of computation
   Benchmark: Knows the language of basic operations

*All standards listed above are from *A Compendium of Standards and Benchmarks for K–12 Education* (Copyright 2004 McREL, www.mcrel.org/standards-benchmarks) Mathematics (Grades 3–5).

Introduction

You just finished teaching a fantastic lesson on probability, and now you need to know, "Do my students get it?" You do not want to give out a worksheet because your students are tired of sitting. Why not try a game to assess the skill?

There is a great need to replace the traditional paper and pencil means of reinforcing math skills with engaging games and activities. *Standards-Based Math Activities & Games* (Grades 3 and 4) is a collection of games that reinforce your math instruction while enabling you to quickly assess your students. Because many of the games are modeled after familiar games, your instructional time is decreased while learning time is increased. These "teacher-friendly" games are designed to connect with any math curriculum while addressing the McREL math standards and benchmarks.

Each math game includes the following components to assist teachers with planning and implementation.

- **Skill:** The math skill is addressed in each game.
- **Standards and Benchmarks:** The standards and benchmarks are taken from *A Compendium of Standards and Benchmarks for K-12 Education* (Copyright 2004 McREL, www.mcrel.org/standards-benchmarks) Mathematics (Grades 3–5).
- **Materials:** The list of materials needed to play the games successfully. Laminate cards, game boards, etc. for durability.
- **Suggested Use:** This area lists the possible ways the game can be implemented.

    Cooperative Groups (Small, independent learning groups of two to four students facilitated by a teacher, teacher's aide, parent, etc.)

    Home Connection (A school-to-home link enabling parents to become involved in their child's learning by reinforcing skills taught at school.)

    Teacher Led (The teacher leads the students in a whole-group game or activity.)

    Tutorial (This is one-on-one instruction with a teacher or teacher's aide providing the student with additional practice of the skill.)

    Centers (The student independently plays the game reinforcing the previously taught skill.)

- **Directions:** This lists detailed and easy-to-follow instructions on how to play the game and how it is to be used by teachers, parents, volunteers, etc.
- **Variations:** This area lists additional ideas on how to use the game.
- **Reminder:** This area lists quick and helpful definitions of the targeted skill with examples.

Addition Bowling

Skill: addition with or without regrouping

Standard: uses basic and advanced procedures while performing the processes of computation

Benchmark: performs basic mental computations

Materials
- a copy of Addition Bowling score sheet for each game played
- Addition Bowling game cards
- Addition Bowling game key
- paper and pencil

Suggested Use
- cooperative groups
- centers
- home connection
- tutorial

Directions (2–4 players)

1. Place the Addition Bowling game cards face down as a draw pile between the players.
2. Players write their names on the score sheet.
3. Player A draws two Addition Bowling game cards from the draw pile.
4. Using mental math or paper and pencil method, Player A adds the two numbers.
5. Player A states the sum (answer) and uses the game key to find how many pins (points) to record on the score sheet. (*Note:* Players check each other's answers before scoring.)
6. Player A places the cards on the bottom of the draw pile.
7. It is then the next player's turn.
8. Game continues until each player has 10 turns.
9. Each player totals his or her points on the score sheet. The player with the most points wins.

Reminder

When the numbers are added together, the answer is called the sum.

Addition Bowling Score Sheet

Players' Names	1	2	3	4	5	6	7	8	9	10	TOTAL

Addition Bowling Score Sheet

Players' Names	1	2	3	4	5	6	7	8	9	10	TOTAL

Addition Bowling (Game Cards)

#8719 Standards-Based Activities & Games

Addition Bowling (Game Cards)

#8719 Standards-Based Activities & Games ©Teacher Created Resources, Inc.

Addition Bowling Game Key

SUM	NUMBER OF PINS
0–100	gutter ball = 0
101–200	1
201–300	2
301–400	3
401–500	4
501–600	5
601–700	6
701–800	7
801–900	8
901–1,000	9
over 1,000	Strike! = 10

- -

Addition Bowling Game Key

SUM	NUMBER OF PINS
0–100	gutter ball = 0
101–200	1
201–300	2
301–400	3
401–500	4
501–600	5
601–700	6
701–800	7
801–900	8
901–1,000	9
over 1,000	Strike! = 10

#8719 Standards-Based Activities & Games — ©Teacher Created Resources, Inc.

Big Money Math

Skill: addition, subtraction, multiplication, division; solving algebraic problems
Standard: understands and applies basic and advanced properties of functions and algebra
Benchmark: knows that a variable is a letter or symbol that stands for one or more numbers
Benchmark: understands the basic concept of an equality relationship (i.e., an equation is a number sentence that shows two quantities that are equal)
Benchmark: solves simple open sentences involving operations on whole numbers (e.g., ? + 17 = 23)

Materials

- Big Money Math answer key
- Big Money Math game cards
- Big Money Math game board (one for each player)
- game markers (counters, buttons, chips)

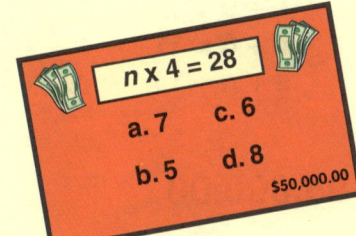

Suggested Use

- cooperative groups
- centers
- home connection
- tutorial

Directions (2 players)

1. Each player chooses a Big Money Math game board.
2. Separate Big Money Math game cards in draw piles according to money amounts. (*Note to Teacher:* Put each set of game cards in envelopes or plastic baggies marked $100.00, $500.00, etc. for storage. Extra game cards are also included to write your own problems.)
3. Player A starts by drawing the top card of the $100.00 draw pile. The player states the correct answer to the problem. Player B checks the answer key for the correct answer. If correct, Player A places his or her game marker on the $100.00 space on the Big Money Math game board, and it is the next player's turn. If the answer given is incorrect, Player A does not move his or her game marker, and the turn goes to the next player. The drawn card is placed at the bottom of the $100.00 draw pile. Player A must again draw from the top of the $100.00 draw pile on his or her next turn.
4. It is then Player B's turn to draw and answer a $100.00 game card.
5. Players continue drawing cards from $500.00, $1,000.00, etc. draw piles until one player reaches the $1,000,000 space.

Reminder

An <u>equality relationship</u> is a number sentence showing two equal quantities.
Example: $54 - n = 13$

Big Money Math (Answer Key)

$100.00

7 + *n* = 13	c.
8 + *n* = 17	a.
n + 0 = 11	d.
n + 9 = 15	b.
n + 6 = 11	a.
8 + *n* = 14	c.

$500.00

n – 5 = 9	b.
n – 5 = 8	a.
14 – *n* = 9	b.
n – 7 = 4	d.
n – 8 = 7	b.
10 – *n* = 8	c.

$1,000.00

16 – *n* = 9	a.
13 – *n* = 8	b.
17 – *n* = 9	d.
12 – *n* = 4	d.
15 – *n* = 9	c.
14 – *n* = 8	c.

$5,000.00

2,000 + *n* + 70 + 8 = 2,578	c.
n + 300 + 60 + 4 = 7,364	d.
9,000 + 800 + *n* + 0 = 9,850	b.
1,000 + 400 + 30 + *n* = 1,436	c.
n + 600 + 40 + 3 = 8,643	a.
3,000 + *n* + 20 + 5 = 3,725	a.

$10,000.00

n + 17 = 23	b.
31 + *n* = 44	d.
n + 60 = 97	a.
56 + *n* = 72	d.
n + 48 = 98	c.
74 + *n* = 83	a.

$50,000.00

7 x *n* = 63	b.
n x 8 = 64	a.
3 x *n* = 27	d.
n x 9 = 54	c.
6 x *n* = 48	d.
n x 4 = 28	a.

$100,000.00

56 ÷ *n* = 8	d.
n ÷ 9 = 6	c.
36 ÷ 6 = *n*	b.
63 ÷ *n* = 9	a.
n ÷ 7 = 3	c.
48 ÷ 6 = *n*	d.

$500,000.00

62 – *n* = 37	b.
40 – *n* = 13	a.
71 – 32 = *n*	d.
54 – *n* = 13	c.
83 – *n* = 78	b.
95 – 67 = *n*	d.

$1,000,000.00

8 + *n* > 10	d.
23 < *n* + 14	a.
7 x *n* < 30	c.
16 + 5 < *n*	a.
36 < 27 + *n*	b.
24 ÷ *n* > 5	a.

Big Money Math (Game Cards)

Card 1 ($100.00): $n + 0 = 11$
a. 10 b. 0 c. 12 d. 11

Card 2 ($100.00): $8 + n = 14$
a. 7 b. 5 c. 6 d. 8

Card 3 ($500.00): $14 - n = 9$
a. 7 b. 5 c. 6 d. 8

Card 4 ($500.00): $10 - n = 8$
a. 1 b. 4 c. 2 d. 3

Card 5 ($100.00): $8 + n = 17$
a. 9 b. 10 c. 8 d. 7

Card 6 ($100.00): $n + 6 = 11$
a. 5 b. 4 c. 6 d. 7

Card 7 ($500.00): $n - 5 = 8$
a. 13 b. 15 c. 14 d. 16

Card 8 ($500.00): $n - 8 = 7$
a. 16 b. 15 c. 18 d. 14

Card 9 ($100.00): $7 + n = 13$
a. 7 b. 5 c. 6 d. 8

Card 10 ($100.00): $n + 9 = 15$
a. 5 b. 6 c. 7 d. 9

Card 11 ($500.00): $n - 5 = 9$
a. 16 b. 14 c. 15 d. 17

Card 12 ($500.00): $n - 7 = 4$
a. 10 b. 14 c. 12 d. 11

Big Money Math (Game Cards)

Card 1: 17 − n = 9 a. 7 b. 5 c. 6 d. 8 $1,000.00

Card 2: 14 − n = 8 a. 7 b. 5 c. 6 d. 8 $1,000.00

Card 3: 9,000 + 800 + n + 0 = 9,850 a. 800 b. 50 c. 500 d. 80 $5,000.00

Card 4: 3,000 + n + 20 + 5 = 3,725 a. 700 b. 200 c. 500 d. 70 $5,000.00

Card 5: 13 − n = 8 a. 7 b. 5 c. 6 d. 8 $1,000.00

Card 6: 15 − n = 9 a. 7 b. 5 c. 6 d. 8 $1,000.00

Card 7: n + 300 + 60 + 4 = 7,364 a. 700 b. 300 c. 3,000 d. 7,000 $5,000.00

Card 8: n + 600 + 40 + 3 = 8,643 a. 8,000 b. 6,000 c. 800 d. 60 $5,000.00

Card 9: 16 − n = 9 a. 7 b. 5 c. 6 d. 8 $1,000.00

Card 10: 12 − n = 4 a. 7 b. 5 c. 6 d. 8 $1,000.00

Card 11: 2,000 + n + 70 + 8 = 2,578 a. 700 b. 200 c. 500 d. 80 $5,000.00

Card 12: 1,000 + 400 + 30 + n = 1,436 a. 60 b. 3 c. 6 d. 30 $5,000.00

#8719 Standards-Based Activities & Games

Big Money Math (Game Cards)

Green cards ($10,000.00)

n + 60 = 97
a. 37
b. 47
c. 27
d. 17

74 + n = 83
a. 9
b. 7
c. 8
d. 10

31 + n = 44
a. 12
b. 11
c. 23
d. 13

n + 48 = 98
a. 40
b. 60
c. 50
d. 30

n + 17 = 23
a. 5
b. 6
c. 4
d. 7

56 + n = 72
a. 6
b. 5
c. 15
d. 16

Red cards ($50,000.00)

3 x n = 27
a. 8
b. 6
c. 7
d. 9

n x 4 = 28
a. 7
b. 5
c. 6
d. 8

n x 8 = 64
a. 8
b. 9
c. 7
d. 6

6 x n = 48
a. 7
b. 5
c. 6
d. 8

7 x n = 63
a. 8
b. 9
c. 7
d. 6

n x 9 = 54
a. 7
b. 5
c. 6
d. 8

#8719 Standards-Based Activities & Games

Big Money Math (Game Cards)

$36 \div 6 = n$	$48 \div 6 = n$	$71 - 32 = n$	$95 - 67 = n$
a. 7 c. 9	a. 9 c. 6	a. 38 c. 28	a. 37 c. 38
b. 6 d. 8	b. 7 d. 8	b. 49 d. 39	b. 27 d. 28
$100,000.00	$100,000.00	$500,000.00	$500,000.00

$n \div 9 = 6$	$n \div 7 = 3$	$40 - n = 13$	$83 - n = 78$
a. 63 c. 54	a. 24 c. 21	a. 27 c. 17	a. 7 c. 6
b. 56 d. 64	b. 28 d. 27	b. 18 d. 28	b. 5 d. 8
$100,000.00	$100,000.00	$500,000.00	$500,000.00

$56 \div n = 8$	$63 \div n = 9$	$62 - n = 37$	$54 - n = 13$
a. 5 c. 4	a. 7 c. 8	a. 14 c. 24	a. 31 c. 41
b. 6 d. 7	b. 6 d. 9	b. 25 d. 15	b. 30 d. 42
$100,000.00	$100,000.00	$500,000.00	$500,000.00

©Teacher Created Resources, Inc.   #8719 Standards-Based Activities & Games

#8719 Standards-Based Activities & Games

Big Money Math (Game Cards and Blank Game Cards)

7 × n < 30
a. 5   c. 4
b. 6   d. 7
$1,000,000.00

24 ÷ n > 5
a. 3   c. 6
b. 24 d. 8
$1,000,000.00

23 < n + 14
a. 11 c. 9
b. 8   d. 7
$1,000,000.00

36 < 27 + n
a. 7   c. 5
b. 11 d. 9
$1,000,000.00

8 + n > 10
a. 1   c. 0
b. 2   d. 3
$1,000,000.00

16 + 5 < n
a. 22 c. 21
b. 20 d. 19
$1,000,000.00

©Teacher Created Resources, Inc.

#8719 Standards-Based Activities & Games

©Teacher Created Resources, Inc.

Big Money Math (Game Boards)

Big Money Math WINNER!

- $1,000,000.00
- $500,000.00
- $100,000.00
- $50,000.00
- $10,000.00
- $5,000.00
- $1,000.00
- $500.00
- $100.00

Big Money Math WINNER!

- $1,000,000.00
- $500,000.00
- $100,000.00
- $50,000.00
- $10,000.00
- $5,000.00
- $1,000.00
- $500.00
- $100.00

©Teacher Created Resources, Inc. #8719 Standards-Based Activities & Games

#8719 Standards-Based Activities & Games

Get to the Point

Skill: decimals

Standard: understands and applies basic and advanced properties of the concepts of numbers

Benchmark: understands the relative magnitude and relationships among whole numbers, fractions, decimals, and mixed numbers

Materials

- Get to the Point game board
- Get to the Point game cards
- a copy of Get to the Point recording sheet for each player
- Get to the Point goal cards
- marker, crayon, or colored pencil

Suggested Use

- cooperative groups
- centers
- home connection
- teacher led
- tutorial

Directions (2 players)

1. Get to the Point game cards are placed face down in a draw pile.
2. Goal cards are placed face down in another draw pile.
3. Each player receives a Get to the Point recording sheet.
4. Player A places the Get to the Point game board in front of him or her. Player A draws four Get to the Point game cards and one Get to the Point goal card. Player A arranges his or her game cards on the game board using addition or subtraction to get as close as possible to the number on the goal card. For example, if Player A draws 1, 7, 6 and 5 game cards and an 8 goal card, Player A would arrange the cards using addition on the game board to achieve the sum of 8.2. The answer is .2 away from the goal of 8.

(Directions continued on next page.)

Get to the Point (cont.)

Directions (cont.)

5. Player A records problem, answer, goal, and difference on his or her Get to the Point recording sheet. In the example mentioned previously, Player A would record as shown below.

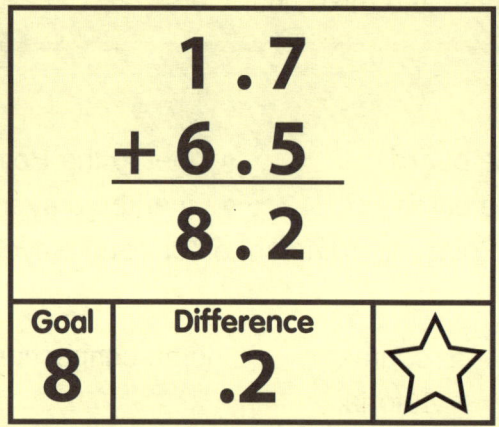

6. It is then Player B's turn. Player B draws four Get to the Point game cards and one Get to the Point goal card. Player B arranges his or her game cards using addition or subtraction to achieve a sum or difference close to the number on the goal card.
7. Player B records the problem, answer, goal, and difference on his or her Get to the Point recording sheet.
8. The player who obtains a sum or difference closest to their goal, colors in the star in that box.
9. Playing cards and goal cards are reshuffled and placed in the bottom of the draw piles.
10. Play continues until one player has five colored stars.

Variations
- Use the free cards as "Wild Cards" (any number determined by the players).
- Use the recording sheet as an assessment.
- Make transparency cards to be used as a teacher-led activity on the overhead.

Reminder

A <u>decimal</u> is a number with one or more digits to the right of the decimal point.
Examples: .3 = 3/10   .25 = ¼

Get to the Point (Recording Sheet)

Round 1			Round 2			Round 3		
Goal	Difference	☆	Goal	Difference	☆	Goal	Difference	☆

Round 4			Round 5			Round 6		
Goal	Difference	☆	Goal	Difference	☆	Goal	Difference	☆

Round 7			Round 8			Round 9		
Goal	Difference	☆	Goal	Difference	☆	Goal	Difference	☆

Round 10			Round 11			Round 12		
Goal	Difference	☆	Goal	Difference	☆	Goal	Difference	☆

Get to the Point (Game Board)

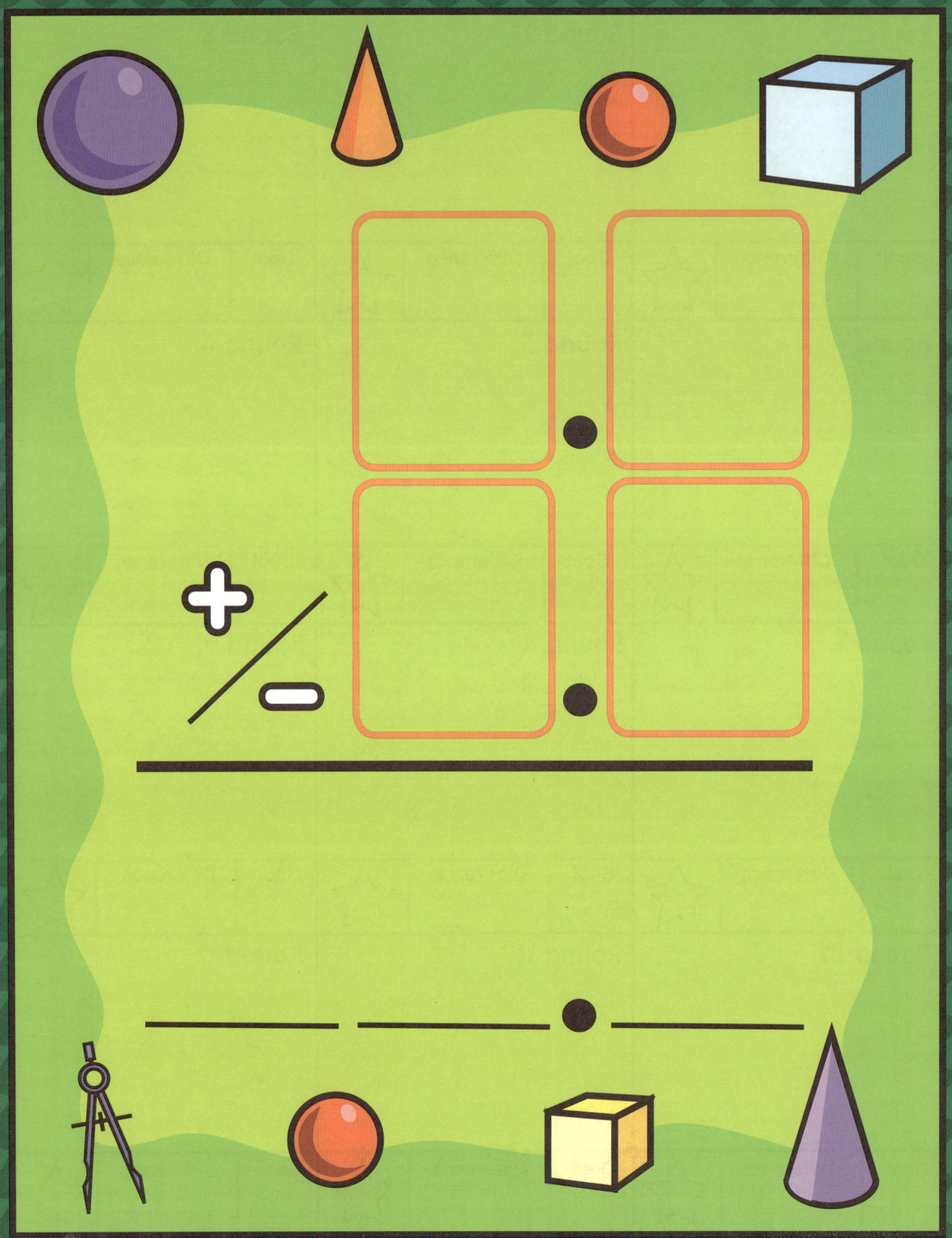

Get to the Point (Goal Cards)

GOAL CARD	GOAL CARD	GOAL CARD
1	**2**	**3**
GOAL CARD	GOAL CARD	GOAL CARD
4	**5**	**6**
GOAL CARD	GOAL CARD	GOAL CARD
7	**8**	**9**

#8719 Standards-Based Activities & Games ©Teacher Created Resources, Inc.

Get to the Point (Game Cards)

©Teacher Created Resources, Inc. #8719 Standards-Based Activities & Games

#8719 Standards-Based Activities & Games 34 ©Teacher Created Resources, Inc.

Place Your Order

Skill: ordering, decimals, fractions, mixed numbers
Standard: understands and applies basic and advanced properties of the concepts of numbers
Benchmark: understands the relative magnitude and relationships among whole numbers, fractions, decimals, and mixed numbers

Materials
- a copy of Place Your Order game board for each player
- Place Your Order game cards
- Place Your Order answer key

Suggested Use
- cooperative groups
- centers
- home connection
- tutorial

Directions (2 players)

1. Put the Place Your Order game cards in a draw pile between players.
2. Each player receives a Place Your Order game board.
3. Player A draws a card and determines where to place it on his or her game board with the goal of having cards in order from least to greatest. For example, if a .2 is drawn, the player would place the card further to the least (left) side. If a 3.2 is drawn, the player would place the card further to the greater (right) side. If a card does not fit into the player's sequence of least to greatest, the drawn card must be placed face down on one of the open spaces on the game board. Once a card has been placed, it may not be moved.
4. Game ends when each player's game board is filled. A point is awarded to the player who has the most face-up cards in the correct sequence from least to greatest. Use the answer key to check the sequence. See example below.
5. Play continues until a determined number of points are reached.

Reminder

<u>Fractions:</u> A number that names part of a whole or group. Example: 1/3
<u>Decimals:</u> A number that uses place value and a decimal point to show tenths and hundredths. Example: 4.5
<u>Mixed Numbers:</u> A number that has a whole number part and a fraction part. Example: 3 ¼

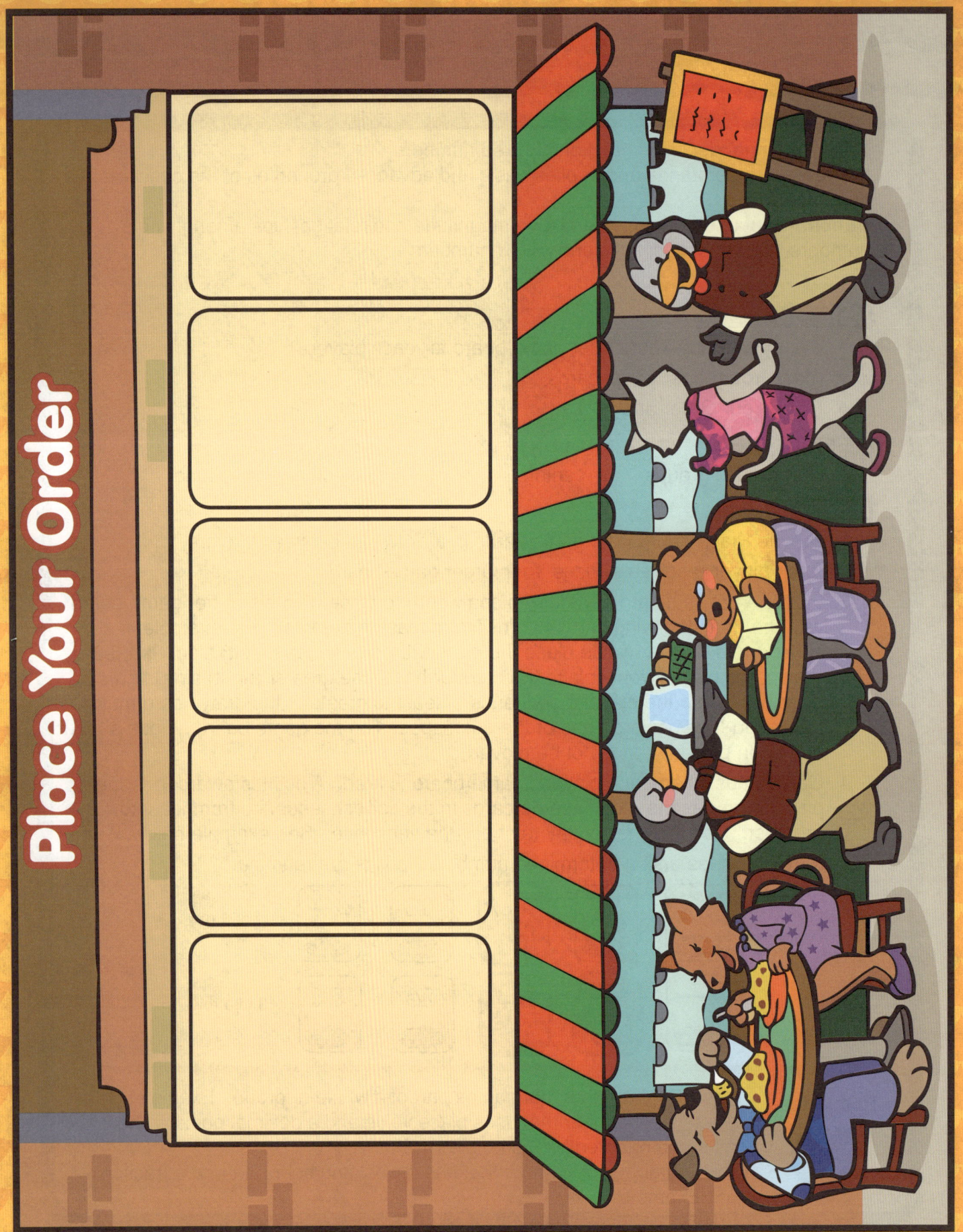

Place Your Order (Game Cards)

#8719 Standards-Based Activities & Games

Place Your Order (Game Cards)

#8719 Standards-Based Activities & Games 40 ©Teacher Created Resources, Inc.

Place Your Order Answer Key

LEAST

.1
.2
3/10
.4
5/10
6/10
.7
eight tenths
.9
1 2/10
1.3
1 5/10
1.6
2.2
2.5
two and seven tenths
2 8/10
3.4
3 6/10
three and eight tenths
4.2
4.7
4 9/10
five and four tenths
5.8
6 9/10
7.2
8 4/10
eight and nine tenths
9.6

GREATEST

#8719 Standards-Based Activities & Games   42   ©Teacher Created Resources, Inc.

M.A.T.H.

Skill: whole number division

Standard: understands and applies basic and advanced properties of the concepts of numbers

Benchmark: understands basic number theory concepts

Materials
- a copy of M.A.T.H. game board for each player
- M.A.T.H. game cards
- M.A.T.H. answer key
- pencil and paper

Suggested Use
- cooperative groups
- centers
- home connection
- tutorial

Directions (2–4 players)

1. Each player receives a M.A.T.H. game board.
2. Place M.A.T.H. cards face down in a draw pile between players.
3. Players take turns drawing cards, answering the division problems, and marking the answer on the M.A.T.H. game board with the goal of spelling "M.A.T.H." in order. If a correct answer is given, the player draws a diagonal line on the correct answer on the M.A.T.H. game board, discards the card, and it is the next player's turn. If there is no matching answer or an incorrect answer is given, the player loses that turn and returns the game card to the bottom of the draw pile. If a "Free Letter" card is drawn, the player moves on to the next letter in spelling "M.A.T.H."
4. The first player to cross out the letters spelling "M.A.T.H." receives 1 point, records the point on a separate sheet of paper, and draws diagonal lines making Xs across the correct answer boxes. The player then begins again to spell "M.A.T.H." with the remaining open boxes.
5. Play continues until all cards have been used. The player with the most points wins.

Reminder

Division: The process of sharing items to find out how many groups can be made or how many items will be in each group; the opposite of multiplication.
Example: $24 \div 6 = 4$

M.A.T.H.

M.A.T.H. (Game Board)

M 10	T 2	A 5	T 10	H 6	A 3
H 8	M 9	T 1	A 6	M 4	H 5
A 2	H 7	A 9	M 3	T 8	H 5
M 7	T 4	H 1	A 6	M 9	T 2
A 4	H 4	T 5	M 1	A 1	M 2
H 9	A 3	M 8	T 7	H 2	A 10

#8719 Standards-Based Activities & Games ©Teacher Created Resources, Inc.

M.A.T.H. (Game Cards)

 81 ÷ 9
 45 ÷ 5
 32 ÷ 4
 56 ÷ 8

 60 ÷ 6
 27 ÷ 3
 56 ÷ 7
 49 ÷ 7

 90 ÷ 9
 54 ÷ 6
 64 ÷ 8
 14 ÷ 2

 100 ÷ 10
 63 ÷ 7
 24 ÷ 3
 63 ÷ 9

#8719 Standards-Based Activities & Games 46 ©Teacher Created Resources, Inc.

M.A.T.H. (Game Cards)

 25 ÷ 5	 45 ÷ 9	 12 ÷ 3	 22 ÷ 11
 48 ÷ 8	 10 ÷ 2	 28 ÷ 7	 27 ÷ 9
 30 ÷ 5	 55 ÷ 11	 32 ÷ 8	 33 ÷ 11
 36 ÷ 6	 35 ÷ 7	 24 ÷ 6	 9 ÷ 3

#8719 Standards-Based Activities & Games   48   ©Teacher Created Resources, Inc.

M.A.T.H. (Game Cards and Blank Game Cards)

#8719 Standards-Based Activities & Games ©Teacher Created Resources, Inc.

M.A.T.H. (Answer Key)

100 ÷ 10 = 10
90 ÷ 9 = 10
60 ÷ 6 = 10
81 ÷ 9 = 9
63 ÷ 7 = 9
54 ÷ 6 = 9
27 ÷ 3 = 9
45 ÷ 5 = 9
24 ÷ 3 = 8
64 ÷ 8 = 8
56 ÷ 7 = 8
32 ÷ 4 = 8
63 ÷ 9 = 7
14 ÷ 2 = 7
49 ÷ 7 = 7
56 ÷ 8 = 7
36 ÷ 6 = 6
30 ÷ 5 = 6
48 ÷ 8 = 6
25 ÷ 5 = 5

35 ÷ 7 = 5
55 ÷ 11 = 5
10 ÷ 2 = 5
45 ÷ 9 = 5
24 ÷ 6 = 4
32 ÷ 8 = 4
28 ÷ 7 = 4
12 ÷ 3 = 4
9 ÷ 3 = 3
33 ÷ 11 = 3
27 ÷ 9 = 3
22 ÷ 11 = 2
10 ÷ 5 = 2
20 ÷ 10 = 2
6 ÷ 3 = 2
18 ÷ 9 = 2
100 ÷ 100 = 1
60 ÷ 60 = 1
10 ÷ 10 = 1
50 ÷ 50 = 1

#8719 Standards-Based Activities & Games   52   ©Teacher Created Resources, Inc.

Time Flies

Skill: elapsed time
Standard: understands and applies basic and advanced properties of the concepts of measurement
Benchmark: Understands relationships between measures

Materials
- Time Flies answer key
- Time Flies game board
- Time Flies game cards
- game markers (counters, buttons, etc.)

Suggested Use
- cooperative groups
- home connection
- centers
- tutorial

Directions (2–4 players)

1. Place the Time Flies game board between players. Place Time Flies game cards face down as a draw pile on the game board.
2. Player A draws the top card from the draw pile and states the elapsed time.
3. Player B checks the answer key for the correct answer.
4. If correct, Player A moves the number of spaces indicated on the card, and it is the next player's turn.
5. If incorrect, the play goes to the next player.
6. If a player draws a "Skip A Turn," "Go Back 2 Spaces," or "Go Back 1 Space" card, the player must do as indicated on the card. Drawn cards go to the bottom of the draw pile.
7. Play continues until one player's game marker lands on the "You have landed!" space.

Reminder

Elapsed time is the amount (period) of time that has elapsed between two points in time.
Example: The elapsed time from 2:45 to 3:00 is 15 minutes.

Time Flies (Answer Key)

1. 2 hours 15 minutes
2. 30 minutes
3. 1 hour 30 minutes
4. 45 minutes
5. 35 minutes
6. 5 hours
7. 1 hour 45 minutes
8. 45 minutes
9. 1 hour 30 minutes
10. 40 minutes
11. 2 hours 30 minutes
12. 2 hours 45 minutes
13. 50 minutes
14. 20 minutes
15. 3 hours 30 minutes
16. 4 hours 15 minutes
17. 35 minutes
18. 1 hour 45 minutes
19. 1 hour 45 minutes
20. 50 minutes
21. 3 hours
22. 2 hours 15 minutes
23. 4 hours 30 minutes
24. 35 minutes
25. 30 minutes
26. 3 hours 15 minutes
27. 4 hours 15 minutes
28. 1 hour 15 minutes
29. 30 minutes
30. 2 hours 45 minutes
31. 3 hours 30 minutes
32. 3 hours 45 minutes
33. 45 minutes

#8719 Standards-Based Activities & Games

Time Flies (Game Cards)

1 8:00 to 10:15 move ahead 4 spaces	**2** 12:15 to 12:45 move ahead 1 space	**3** 9:30 to 11:00 move ahead 3 spaces
4 3:15 to 4:00 move ahead 2 spaces	**5** 7:35 to 8:10 move ahead 3 spaces	**6** 5:30 to 10:30 move ahead 1 space
7 6:15 to 8:00 move ahead 3 spaces	**8** 7:25 to 8:10 move ahead 2 spaces	**9** 8:45 to 10:15 move ahead 4 spaces
10 1:10 to 1:50 move ahead 1 space	**11** 2:30 to 5:00 move ahead 3 spaces	**12** 10:45 to 1:30 move ahead 4 spaces
13 6:05 to 6:55 move ahead 2 spaces	**14** 9:25 to 9:45 move ahead 1 space	**15** 12:00 to 3:30 move ahead 3 spaces
16 4:15 to 8:30 move ahead 5 spaces	**17** 5:25 to 6:00 move ahead 2 spaces	**18** 9:45 to 11:30 move ahead 1 space

#8719 Standards-Based Activities & Games

Time Flies (Game Cards)

19 8:15 to 10:00 move ahead 3 spaces	20 11:20 to 12:10 move ahead 2 spaces	21 10:00 to 1:00 move ahead 1 space
22 3:45 to 6:00 move ahead 4 spaces	23 9:15 to 1:45 move ahead 5 spaces	24 2:20 to 2:55 move ahead 2 spaces
25 12:45 to 1:15 move ahead 1 space	26 7:30 to 10:45 move ahead 4 spaces	27 4:45 to 9:00 move ahead 3 spaces
28 5:15 to 6:30 move ahead 2 spaces	29 1:55 to 2:25 move ahead 1 space	30 6:45 to 9:30 move ahead 4 spaces
31 8:30 to 12:00 move ahead 3 spaces	32 11:15 to 3:00 move ahead 4 spaces	33 10:45 to 11:30 move ahead 2 spaces
SKIP A TURN	GO BACK 2 SPACES	GO BACK 1 SPACE

#8719 Standards-Based Activities & Games

Pizza Delivery

Skill: fractions

Standard: understands and applies basic and advanced properties of the concepts of numbers

Benchmark: understands the relative magnitude and relationships among whole numbers, fractions, decimals, and mixed numbers

Materials
- a copy of Pizza Delivery game board for each player
- Pizza Delivery game spinner (assembled as instructed)
- Pizza Delivery game pieces

Suggested Use
- cooperative groups
- centers
- home connection
- tutorial

Directions (2–4 players)

1. Each player receives a Pizza Delivery game board. Pizza slices are placed in four piles between players according to size.
2. The Pizza Delivery game spinner is placed between players.
3. Player A spins the spinner and selects the game piece shown on the spinner to cover an open area on the game board. For example, a player may cover a 1/8 area on the 1/8 circle or cover a 1/8 game area on half of the 1/4 area.
4. Players continue taking turns spinning and covering the Pizza Delivery game board.
5. Game ends when one player has the entire Pizza Delivery game board covered.

Variation
- Players use one game board. Players receive a point when they lay down the last game piece on each circle.

Reminder

A <u>fraction</u> is part of a whole.
Example: 1/8 is one part out of eight equal parts

Pizza Delivery (Game Board)

Pizza Delivery (Game Spinner)

Assembly Instructions

To make the spinner, use a paper clip and a pencil. Place the paper clip in the middle of the spinner and hold it in place with the pencil. Spin the "spinner" (paper clip) as you normally would.

#8719 Standards-Based Activities & Games   64   ©Teacher Created Resources, Inc.

Pizza Delivery (Game Pieces)

#8719 Standards-Based Activities & Games ©Teacher Created Resources, Inc.

#8719 Standards-Based Activities & Games

Pizza Delivery (Game Pieces)

©Teacher Created Resources, Inc. #8719 Standards-Based Activities & Games

#8719 Standards-Based Activities & Games

Pizza Delivery (Game Pieces)

71

©Teacher Created Resources, Inc. #8719 Standards-Based Activities & Games

#8719 Standards-Based Activities & Games 72 ©Teacher Created Resources, Inc.

Pizza Delivery (Game Pieces)

#8719 Standards-Based Activities & Games

Pizza Delivery (Game Pieces)

#8719 Standards-Based Activities & Games

Pizza Delivery (Game Pieces)

#8719 Standards-Based Activities & Games   78   ©Teacher Created Resources, Inc.

Pizza Delivery (Game Pieces)

#8719 Standards-Based Activities & Games

Inside and Out

Skill: perimeter and area of a figure
Standard: understands and applies basic and advanced properties of the concepts of measurement
Benchmark: understands the basic measures of perimeter, area, volume, capacity, mass, angle, and circumference

Materials
- a copy of Inside and Out game sheet for each player
- Inside and Out game cards
- colored pencils, markers, or crayons

Suggested Use
- cooperative groups
- home connection
- centers
- tutorial

Directions (2 players)

1. Each player receives an Inside and Out game sheet. Place Inside and Out game cards face up in a draw pile between players.
2. Player A draws the top card of the draw pile. The player states the area and perimeter of the figure on the card and determines which is larger. For example, if a figure is 8 units wide and 2 units high, the area is 16 square units and the perimeter is 20 units. The perimeter of the figure is larger.
3. Player B checks the back of the card for the correct answer. If correct, Player A colors a perimeter space (P) if the perimeter is larger or an area space (A) if the area is larger. If the perimeter and the area are the same, then the player colors a perimeter space and an area space. The card is then placed at the bottom of the draw pile. If the answer given is incorrect, the turn goes to the next player. The card is placed at the bottom of the draw pile.
4. Play continues until one player's Inside and Out game sheet is completely colored.

Reminder

The <u>area</u> of a figure is the number of square units inside the figure. It is the product of the length and width.
Example: The area of the figure is 6 square units.
3 units x 2 units = 6 square units

2 units
3 units

The <u>perimeter</u> of a figure is the distance around the outside of the figure. It is the sum of the lengths of all its sides.
Example: The perimeter of the figure is 10 units.
3 units + 2 units + 3 units + 2 units = 10 units

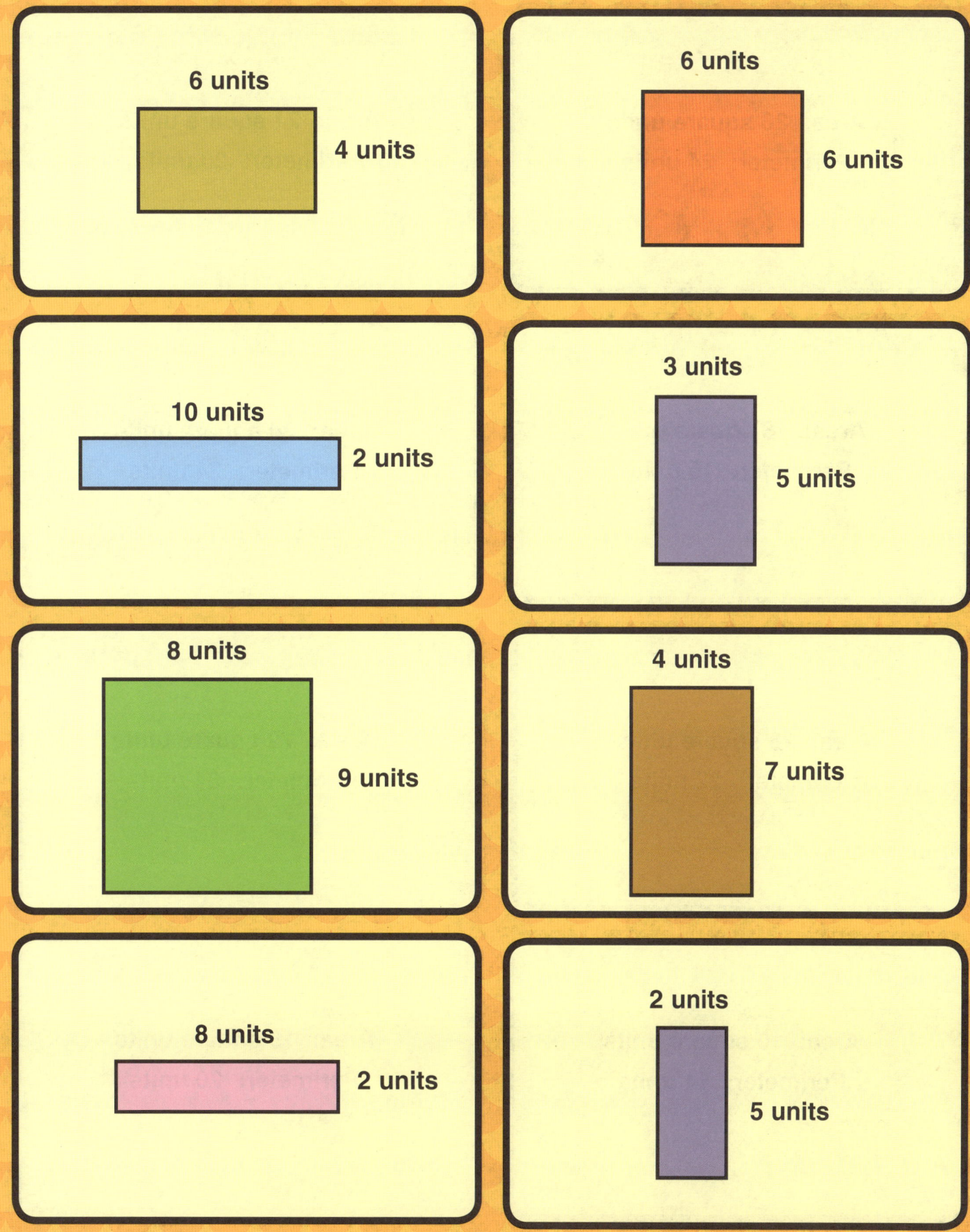

Inside and Out (Game Cards—Back)

Area: 36 square units
Perimeter: 24 units

Area: 24 square units
Perimeter: 20 units

Area: 15 square units
Perimeter: 16 units

Area: 20 square units
Perimeter: 24 units

Area: 28 square units
Perimeter: 22 units

Area: 72 square units
Perimeter: 34 units

Area: 10 square units
Perimeter: 14 units

Area: 16 square units
Perimeter: 20 units

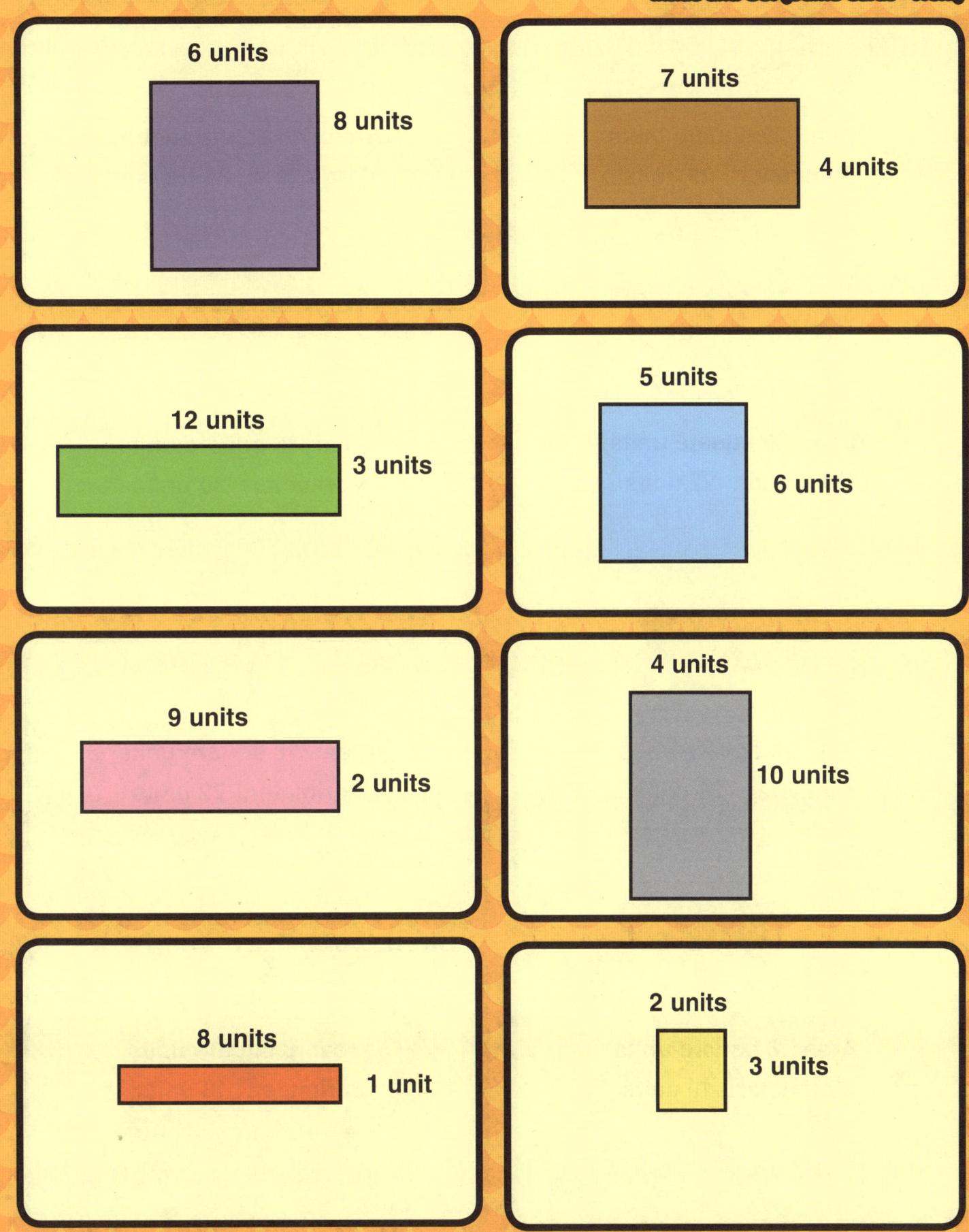

Inside and Out (Game Cards—Back)

Area: 28 square units
Perimeter: 22 units

Area: 48 square units
Perimeter: 28 units

Area: 30 square units
Perimeter: 22 units

Area: 36 square units
Perimeter: 30 units

Area: 40 square units
Perimeter: 28 units

Area: 18 square units
Perimeter: 22 units

Area: 6 square units
Perimeter: 10 units

Area: 8 square units
Perimeter: 18 units

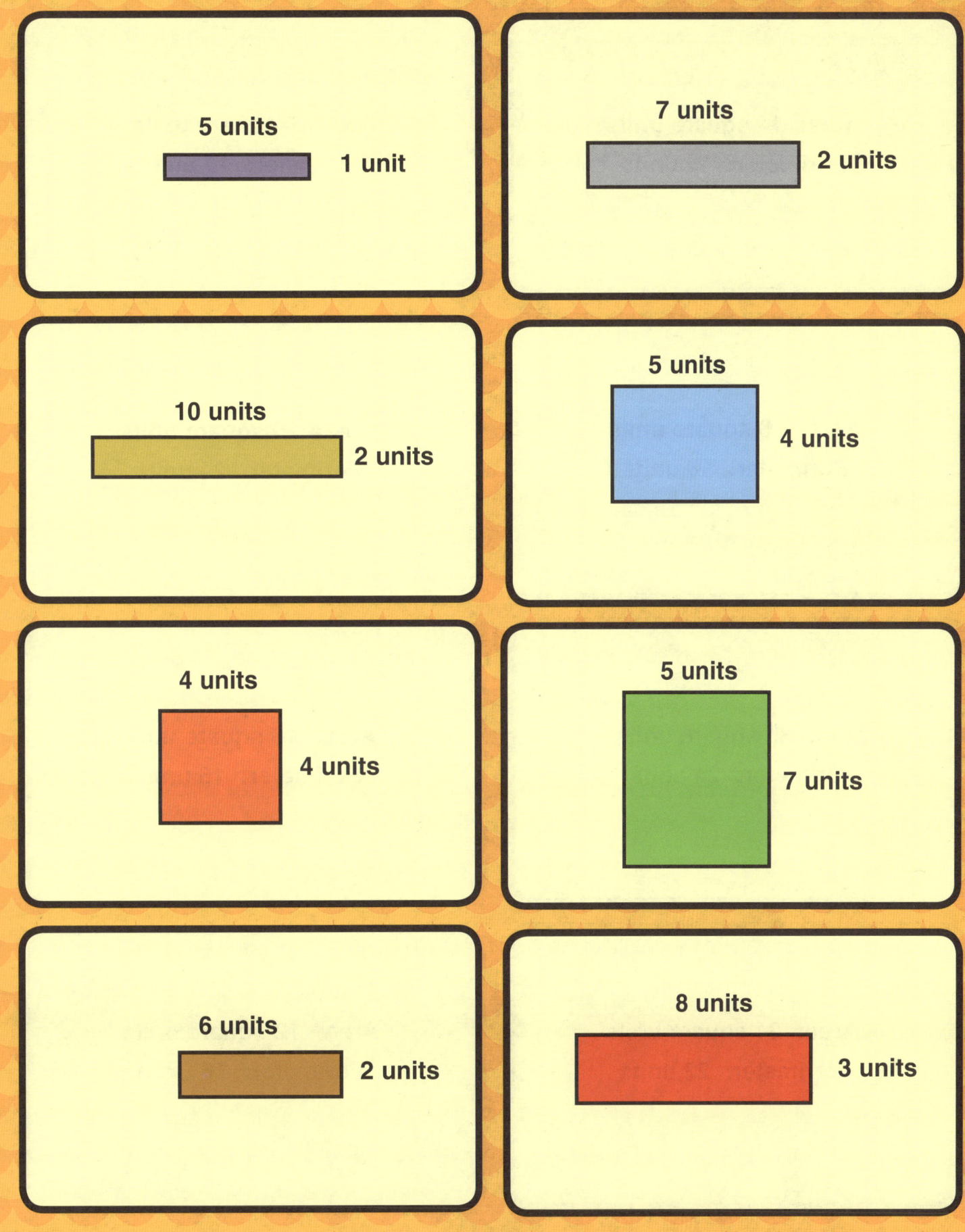

Inside and Out (Game Cards—Back)

Area: 14 square units Perimeter: 18 units	Area: 5 square units Perimeter: 12 units
Area: 20 square units Perimeter: 18 units	Area: 20 square units Perimeter: 24 units
Area: 35 square units Perimeter: 24 units	Area: 16 square units Perimeter: 16 units
Area: 24 square units Perimeter: 22 units	Area: 12 square units Perimeter: 16 units

Fill 'Er Up

Skill: measurement of capacity

Standard: understands and applies basic and advanced properties of the concepts of measurement

Benchmark: understands the basic measures of perimeter, area, volume, capacity, mass, angle, and circumference

Materials
- a copy of Fill 'Er Up reference chart for each player
- Fill 'Er Up game cards

Suggested Use
- cooperative groups
- centers
- home connection
- tutorial

Directions (3–5 players)

1. One player is chosen as the "milkman." The milkman is responsible for the gallon cards, collected cards, and reference charts. Fill 'Er Up cards are placed face down in a draw pile between players. Each player receives a reference chart.
2. Player A draws a card from the draw pile and lays it face up in front of him or her. Players continue drawing cards and placing them face up in front of them.
3. On his or her turn, a player may exchange his or her cards for a gallon card from the milkman when he or she has cards adding up to one gallon.
4. If a player draws a Trade a Card, he or she may save the card and trade it for another player's card whenever it is his or her turn. The milkman collects the Trade a Card after it has been used.
5. If a player draws a Take a Player's Card, he or she may take a card from any player, or the Take a Player's Card may be saved and used later when it is that player's turn. The milkman collects the Take a Player's Card after it has been used. A gallon card cannot be traded or taken from a player.
6. When all the cards have been drawn from the draw pile, the milkman shuffles and restocks the draw pile with the collected cards. Game ends when a player collects three gallon cards.

Variations
- Use only pint and quart cards.
- The game is played with only the milkman using the reference chart.
- Play without using the Trade a Card and/or Take a Player's Card.

Reminder

Capacity is the amount of dry or liquid measure in a container.
Example: 2 cups = 1 pint

Fill 'Er Up Reference Chart

Gallon

Quart		Quart		Quart		Quart	
Pint	Pint	Pint	Pint	Pint	Pint	Pint	Pint
Cup Cup	Cup Cup	Cup Cup	Cup Cup	Cup Cup	Cup Cup	Cup Cup	Cup Cup

Fill 'Er Up Reference Chart

Gallon

Quart		Quart		Quart		Quart	
Pint	Pint	Pint	Pint	Pint	Pint	Pint	Pint
Cup Cup	Cup Cup	Cup Cup	Cup Cup	Cup Cup	Cup Cup	Cup Cup	Cup Cup

Fill 'Er Up (Game Cards)

TAKE A PLAYER'S CARD	TAKE A PLAYER'S CARD	TAKE A PLAYER'S CARD
TRADE A CARD	TRADE A CARD	TRADE A CARD

1 CUP

1 CUP

1 CUP

1 CUP

1 CUP

1 CUP

#8719 Standards-Based Activities & Games 92 ©Teacher Created Resources, Inc.

Fill 'Er Up (Game Cards)

 1 CUP
 1 CUP
 1 CUP
 1 CUP
 1 CUP
 1 CUP
 1 CUP
 1 CUP
 1 CUP
 1 CUP
 1 CUP
 1 CUP

#8719 Standards-Based Activities & Games 94 ©Teacher Created Resources, Inc.

Fill 'Er Up (Game Cards)

#8719 Standards-Based Activities & Games

Fill 'Er Up (Game Cards)

1 GALLON

1 GALLON

1 GALLON

1 GALLON

1 GALLON

1 GALLON

1 GALLON

1 GALLON

1 GALLON

1 GALLON

1 GALLON

1 GALLON

#8719 Standards-Based Activities & Games ©Teacher Created Resources, Inc.

Fill 'Er Up (Game Cards)

1 PINT

1 PINT

1 PINT

1 PINT

1 PINT

1 PINT

1 PINT

1 PINT

1 PINT

1 PINT

1 PINT

1 PINT

©Teacher Created Resources, Inc. 99 #8719 Standards-Based Activities & Games

#8719 Standards-Based Activities & Games 100 ©Teacher Created Resources, Inc.

Ounce or Pound?

Skill: measurement

Standard: understands and applies basic and advanced properties of the concepts of measurement

Benchmark: understands relationships between measures

Materials
- a copy of Ounce or Pound? game sheet for each player
- dice
- pencil, crayon, etc.

Suggested Use
- cooperative groups
- home connection
- centers
- tutorial

Directions (2 players)

1. Player A rolls two dice to find the number of ounces (rolling a 5 and a 4 equals 54 ounces).
2. Player A then rolls one die to find the number of pounds (rolling a 2 equals 2 pounds).
3. Player A records both amounts on the Ounce or Pound? game sheet.
4. Player A checks the math key. If the ounces are greater, the player receives 1 point; if the pounds are greater, the player receives 2 points. If the amounts are equal, the player receives 3 points.
5. Players continue taking turns as described above. The player with the most points after 6 rounds, wins.

Reminder One pound equals 16 ounces.
A slice of bread weighs about 1 ounce.
A loaf of bread weighs about 1 pound.

Ounce or Pound? (Game Sheet)

Ounce or Pound?

	Number of Ounces	Number of Pounds	Score
Roll 1			
Roll 2			
Roll 3			
Roll 4			
Roll 5			
Roll 6			

* Ounces greater = 1 point
* Pounds greater = 2 points
* Equal amounts = 3 points

Total = _____

MATH KEY
1 lb. = 16 oz.
2 lbs. = 32 oz.
3 lbs. = 48 oz.
4 lbs. = 64 oz.
5 lbs. = 80 oz.
6 lbs. = 96 oz.

Powerful Patterns

Skill: number patterns

Standard: understands and applies basic and advanced properties of functions and algebra

Benchmark: recognizes a wide variety of patterns and the rules that explain them

Materials
- Powerful Patterns answer key
- Powerful Patterns pattern cards
- Powerful Patterns game cards

Suggested Use
- cooperative groups
- centers
- home connection
- tutorial

Directions (2 players)

1. Each player receives three Powerful Patterns pattern cards. Players place pattern cards face up in front of them.
2. Powerful Patterns game cards are placed face down as a draw pile, while the top card is turned over to start the discard pile.
3. Player A draws from either the draw or discard pile and uses or places the card in the discard pile.
4. Player A checks his or her cards for a Powerful Patterns set. A Powerful Patterns set includes a matching pattern card, rule card, and missing number card. For example:

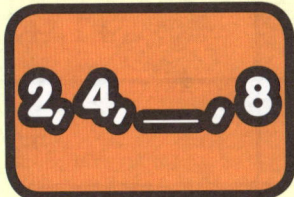  

5. If a player makes a Powerful Patterns set, the set is checked using the answer key and the set is turned over.
6. It is then Player B's turn. Player B draws a card from the draw or discard pile.
7. Play continues until one player has three complete Powerful Patterns sets.

Reminder

A <u>number pattern</u> is a series of numbers that follows a rule.
Examples: 1, 3, 5, 7, 9 (rule—add 2)
2, 4, 8, 16, 32 (rule—multiply by 2)

Powerful Patterns (Answer Key)

Pattern	Missing Number	Rule
24, 26, ___, 30	28	+2
24, ___, 32, 36	28	+4
33, 30, ___, 24	27	−3
4, 8, ___, 32	16	x2
28, 24, 20, ___	16	−4
35, ___, 45, 50	40	+5
1, 3, 9, ___	27	x3
___, 41, 43, 46	40	+1, +2, +3
72, 66, ___, 54	60	−6
22, 23, 25, ___	28	+1, +2, +3
8, 12, ___, 20	16	+4
16, 21, ___, 34	27	+5, +6, +7
80, ___, 20, 10	40	÷2
45, 50, 55, ___	60	+5
65, ___, 56, 53	60	−5, −4, −3

Powerful Patterns (Pattern Cards)

8, 12, ___, 20	35, ___, 45, 50	24, 26, ___, 30
16, 21, ___, 34	1, 3, 9, ___	24, ___, 32, 36
80, ___, 20, 10	___, 41, 43, 46	33, 30, ___, 24
65, ___, 56, 53	72, 66, ___, 54	4, 8, ___, 32
45, 50, 55, ___	22, 23, 25, ___	28, 24, 20, ___

#8719 Standards-Based Activities & Games

Powerful Patterns (Game Cards)

+2	+4	−3
×2	−4	+5
×3	+1, +2, +3	−6
+1, +2, +3	+4	+5, +6, +7
÷2	−5, −4, −3	+5

#8719 Standards-Based Activities & Games

Powerful Patterns (Game Cards)

28	28	28
16	16	16
40	40	40
27	27	27
60	60	60

#8719 Standards-Based Activities & Games   110   ©Teacher Created Resources, Inc.

Place Value Victory

Skill: place value

Standard: understands and applies basic and advanced properties of the concepts of numbers

Benchmark: understands the basic meaning of place value

Materials
- a copy of Place Value Victory game sheet for each player
- Place Value Victory game cards
- Place Value Victory answer key
- pencil

Suggested Use
- cooperative groups
- home connection
- centers
- tutorial
- teacher led

Directions (2 to 4 players)

1. Place the Place Value Victory cards face down in a draw pile between players. (*Note to Teacher:* Use only the cards that align with your students' skill level.)
2. Each player receives a Place Value Victory game sheet. (*Note to Teacher:* As an option, make a transparency of the game sheet and play against the class.)
3. Player A chooses the top card of the draw pile. The player states the expanded notation of the number and if correct, writes the value of each number on the Place Value Victory game sheet in the corresponding columns. For example, if 413,751 is drawn, the player states 400,000 + 10,000 + 3,000 + 700 + 50 + 1 and writes the numbers as seen in the example below. If the stated expanded notation is incorrect, the player does not write any number values on the game sheet.
4. Play continues until one player's Place Value Victory game sheet is filled in.
5. Each player totals the value of the numbers in each column on his or her game sheet. The player having the highest total in each column stars that box. The player with the most stars is the winner.

	Hundred Thousands	Ten Thousands	Thousands	Hundreds	Tens	Ones
1	400,000	10,000	3,000	700	50	1
2						
3						

Reminder

Place value is the value given to a digit by its place in a number.
Expanded notation is a way to write a number as the sum of the values of its digits. (Example: 1,256 can be written as 1,000 + 200 + 50 + 6)

Place Value Victory (Game Sheet)

Place Value Round	Hundred Thousands	Ten Thousands	Thousands	Hundreds	Tens	Ones
1						
2						
3						
4						
5						
6						
7						
8						
Total						

Place Value Victory (Game Cards)

184,057	173,296	123,857
238,699	210,576	208,056
337,058	391,100	345,089
491,286	467,028	498,462
522,069	560,287	592,057

#8719 Standards-Based Activities & Games ©Teacher Created Resources, Inc.

Place Value Victory (Game Cards)

12,058	19,057	17,066
29,796	21,123	24,756
37,697	34,811	30,002
41,195	45,337	48,809
56,023	54,467	52,273

Place Value Victory (Game Cards)

1,087	1,866	1,584
2,650	2,947	2,013
3,912	3,950	3,675
4,978	4,253	4,107
5,878	5,294	5,909

#8719 Standards-Based Activities & Games

Place Value Victory (Game Cards)

846	260	781
955	362	439
508	688	736
611	999	177
284	100	565

#8719 Standards-Based Activities & Games

Place Value Victory (Answer Key)

592,057 = 500,000 + 90,000 + 2,000 + 50 + 7
560,287 = 500,000 + 60,000 + 200 + 80 + 7
522,069 = 500,000 + 20,000 + 2,000 + 60 + 9
498,462 = 400,000 + 90,000 + 8,000 + 400 + 60 + 2
491,286 = 400,000 + 90,000 + 1,000 + 200 + 80 + 6
467,028 = 400,000 + 60,000 + 7,000 + 20 + 8
391,100 = 300,000 + 90,000 + 1,000 + 100
345,089 = 300,000 + 40,000 + 5,000 + 80 + 9
337,058 = 300,000 + 30,000 + 7,000 + 50 + 8
238,699 = 200,000 + 30,000 + 8,000 + 600 + 90 + 9
210,576 = 200,000 + 10,000 + 500 + 70 + 6
208,056 = 200,000 + 8,000 + 50 + 6
184,057 = 100,000 + 80,000 + 4,000 + 50 + 7
173,296 = 100,000 + 70,000 + 3,000 + 200 + 90 + 6
123,857 = 100,000 + 20,000 + 3,000 + 800 + 50 + 7
56,023 = 50,000 + 6,000 + 20 + 3
54,467 = 50,000 + 4,000 + 400 + 60 + 7
52,273 = 50,000 + 2,000 + 200 + 70 + 3
48,809 = 40,000 + 8,000 + 800 + 9
45,337 = 40,000 + 5,000 + 300 + 30 + 7
41,195 = 40,000 + 1,000 + 100 + 90 + 5
37,697 = 30,000 + 7,000 + 600 + 90 + 7
34,811 = 30,000 + 4,000 + 800 + 10 + 1
30,002 = 30,000 + 2
29,796 = 20,000 + 9,000 + 700 + 90 + 6
24,756 = 20,000 + 4,000 + 700 + 50 + 6
21,123 = 20,000 + 1,000 + 100 + 20 + 3
19,057 = 10,000 + 9,000 + 50 + 7
17,066 = 10,000 + 7,000 + 60 + 6
12,058 = 10,000 + 2,000 + 50 + 8

5,909 = 5,000 + 900 + 9
5,878 = 5,000 + 800 + 70 + 8
5,294 = 5,000 + 200 + 90 + 4
4,978 = 4,000 + 900 + 70 + 8
4,253 = 4,000 + 200 + 50 + 3
4,107 = 4,000 + 100 + 7
3,950 = 3,000 + 900 + 50
3,912 = 3,000 + 900 + 10 + 2
3,675 = 3,000 + 600 + 70 + 5
2,947 = 2,000 + 900 + 40 + 7
2,650 = 2,000 + 600 + 50
2,013 = 2,000 + 10 + 3
1,866 = 1,000 + 800 + 60 + 6
1,584 = 1,000 + 500 + 80 + 4
1,087 = 1,000 + 80 + 7
999 = 900 + 90 + 9
955 = 900 + 50 + 5
846 = 800 + 40 + 6
781 = 700 + 80 + 1
736 = 700 + 30 + 6
688 = 600 + 80 + 8
611 = 600 + 10 + 1
565 = 500 + 60 + 5
508 = 500 + 8
439 = 400 + 30 + 9
362 = 300 + 60 + 2
284 = 200 + 80 + 4
260 = 200 + 60
177 = 100 + 70 + 7
100 = 100

#8719 Standards-Based Activities & Games

Take a Chance

Skill: probability

Standard: understands and applies basic and advanced concepts of probability

Benchmark: recognizes events that are sure to happen, events that are sure not to happen, and events that may or may not happen (e.g., in terms of "certain," "likely," and "unlikely")

Materials
- Take a Chance game cards

Suggested Use
- cooperative groups
- tutorial
- home connection
- centers

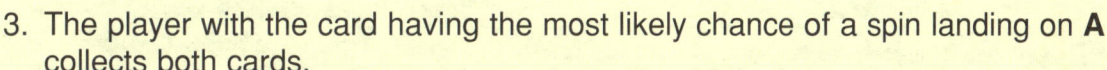

Directions (2 players)

1. Place Take a Chance game cards face down in a draw pile between players.
2. Both players draw a card from the draw pile and lay the cards face up.
3. The player with the card having the most likely chance of a spin landing on **A** collects both cards.
4. If both cards have the same chance of a spin landing on **A**, the cards are placed in a discard pile.
5. Round 1 ends when all cards have been drawn.
6. Cards are reshuffled and placed face down in the draw pile at the end of each round.
7. Round 2 is played with the most likely chance of a spin landing on **B**.
8. Round 3 is played with the most likely chance of a spin landing on **C**. If two cards are drawn and neither player has a **C**, each player keeps his or her drawn card.
9. After Round 3, the player with the most cards is the winner.

Note to Teacher: Review common denominators to compare fractions.

Reminder — <u>Probability</u> is determining how likely an event is to occur. For example, if a spinner has four equal sections and 3 out of the 4 sections are blue, and 1 out of the 4 yellow, it is more likely the spinner will land on blue.

#8719 Standards-Based Activities & Games   124   ©Teacher Created Resources, Inc.

Take a Chance (Game Cards)

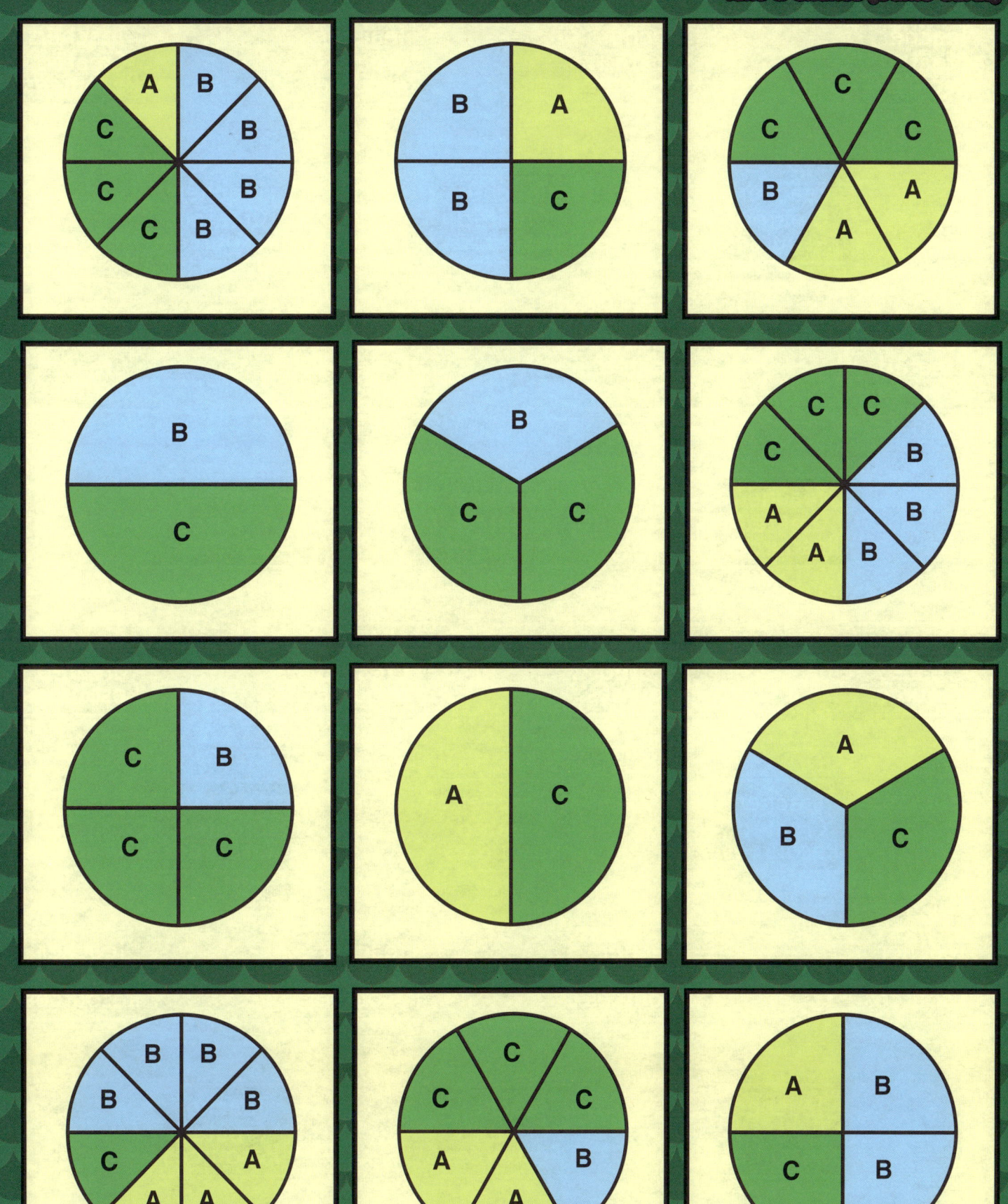

#8719 Standards-Based Activities & Games   126   ©Teacher Created Resources, Inc.

Take a Chance (Game Cards)

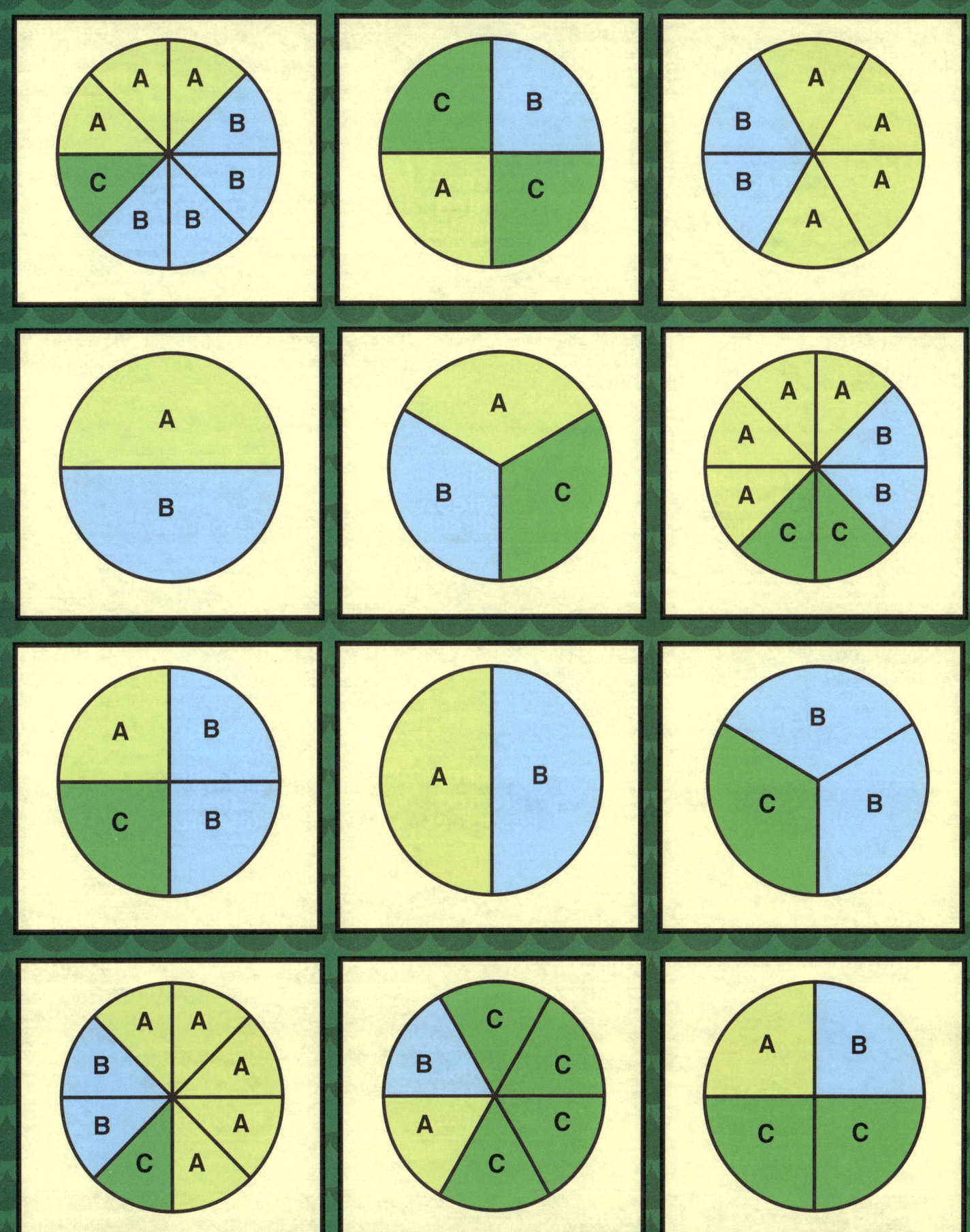

#8719 Standards-Based Activities & Games   128   ©Teacher Created Resources, Inc.

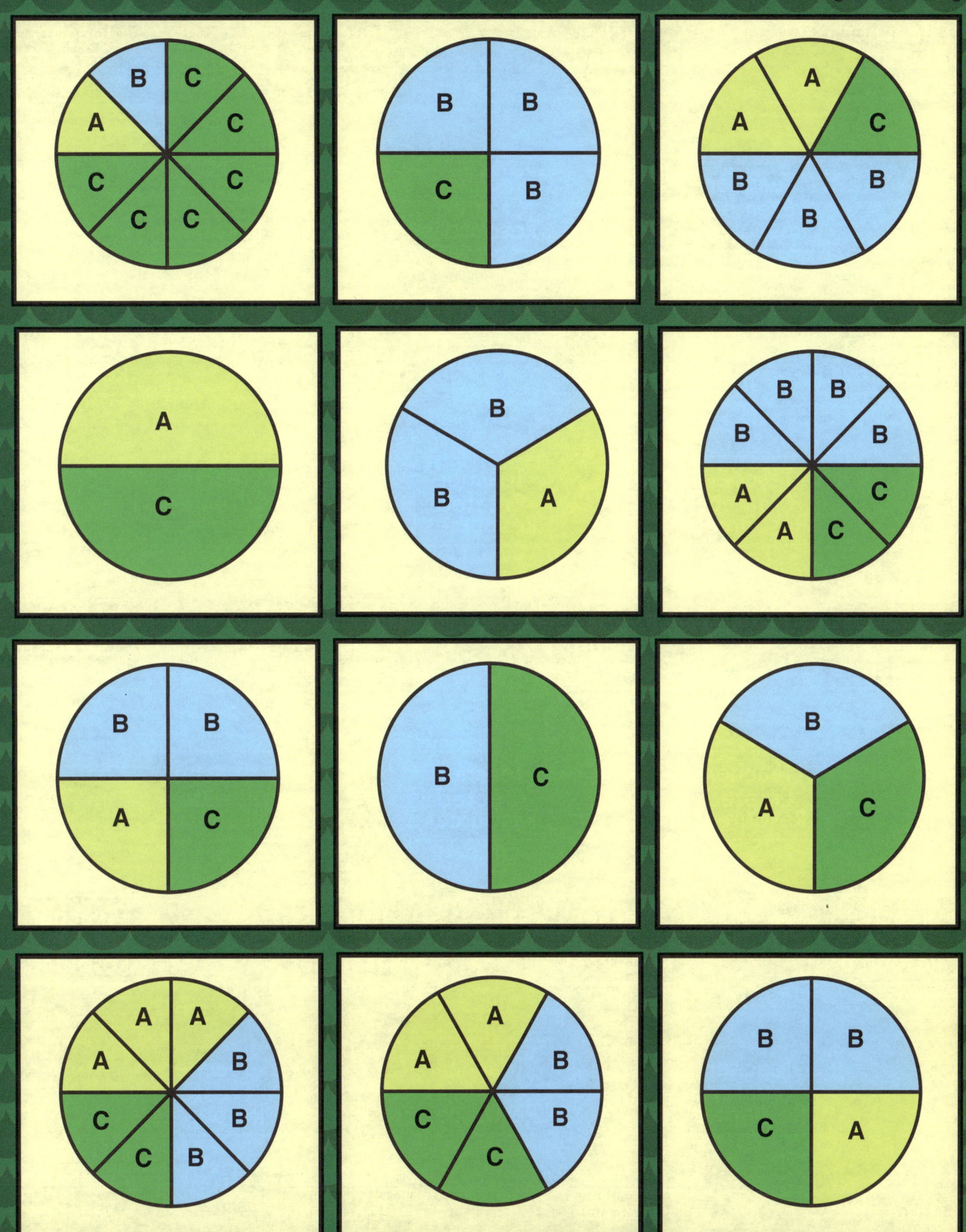

#8719 Standards-Based Activities & Games   130   ©Teacher Created Resources, Inc.

Problem Solving Speedway

Skill: problem solving

Standard: uses a variety of strategies in the problem-solving process

Benchmark: uses a variety of strategies to understand problem situations

Materials
- Problem Solving Speedway game cards
- a copy of Problem Solving Speedway game board for each player
- Problem Solving Speedway answer key
- Problem Solving Speedway game markers (one for each player)

Suggested Use
- cooperative groups
- home connection
- tutorial
- centers

Directions (2 players)

1. Each player receives a Problem Solving Speedway game board and a game marker.
2. Problem Solving Speedway game cards are placed face down between players as a draw pile.
3. Player A chooses a game card and answers the question. Player B checks the answer key. If correct, Player A advances with his or her game marker.
4. If the card states, "Advance 1 space," the player may advance one space on the speedway. If the card states, "Advance 2 spaces," the player may advance two spaces. If the answer is incorrect, the player does not advance on the game board.
5. Players take turns drawing and answering questions, advancing on the game board for correct answers.
6. The first player to make it around the speedway wins the game.

Reminder

These steps can help with problem solving: Read, Plan, Solve, and Look Back.

#8719 Standards-Based Activities & Games 132 ©Teacher Created Resources, Inc.

Problem Solving Speedway (Game Cards)

1. Marge bought 7 candy bars. She has 3 friends, and each of them will receive 2 candy bars. How many candy bars will she have left over?

   A. 2
   B. 1
   C. none

   (ADVANCE 1 SPACE)

2. This year, Mrs. Anderson has 6 fewer students than last year. Last year she had 31 students. Which shows how to solve the problem?

   A. 31 – 6
   B. 31 – 4
   C. 31 + 6

   (ADVANCE 2 SPACES)

3. Madeline bought 3 pencils for $1.75 each and a notebook for $2.50. How much did she pay for the pencils?

   A. $5.50
   B. $5.25
   C. $4.25

   (ADVANCE 1 SPACE)

4. Jena had about 35 marbles until her mother bought her 42 more. Her father then gave her 27 more for her birthday. What is the closest estimate to show how many marbles Jena had?

   A. 90 marbles
   B. 110 marbles
   C. 100 marbles

   (ADVANCE 1 SPACE)

5. Kevin has $5.00. He wants to buy gumballs for 35 cents each. What is the most amount of gumballs Kevin can buy?

   A. 12 gumballs
   B. 10 gumballs
   C. 14 gumballs

   (ADVANCE 2 SPACES)

6. On Sunday 3 cars were rented. On each of the other days of the week, 4 cars were rented. How many cars were rented in all that week?

   A. 17 cars
   B. 22 cars
   C. 27 cars

   (ADVANCE 2 SPACES)

©Teacher Created Resources, Inc.   #8719 Standards-Based Activities & Games

#8719 Standards-Based Activities & Games

Problem Solving Speedway (Game Cards)

---

7. Sue has 4 boxes. Each box has 3 toys in it. Which is the correct mathematical sentence for this problem?

A. 3 + 4
B. 4 + 4
C. 3 + 3 + 3 + 3

(ADVANCE 1 SPACE)

---

8. There are 4 girls and 8 boys playing kickball. Which answer shows how many of the players are girls?

A. 1/3
B. 4 + 8
C. 8 ÷ 4

(ADVANCE 2 SPACES)

---

9. Judy has $20.00. She would like to buy a new sweater and pants. The sweater costs $10.50. Does she have enough money?

A. Yes
B. No
C. Not enough information

(ADVANCE 1 SPACE)

---

10. The Bluejays scored 6 points in the first quarter, 8 points in the second quarter, 6 points in the third quarter, and 5 points in the fourth quarter. Which shows the total number of points?

A. (6 x 2) + 8 + 5
B. (8 x 2) + 6 + 5
C. (5 x 2) + 6 + 8

(ADVANCE 2 SPACES)

---

11. The player with the most points is the winner. Carla scored 46 points, Josh scored 79 points, Mary scored 83 points, and Brooke scored 26 points. Which player came in second?

A. Josh
B. Carla
C. Mary

(ADVANCE 1 SPACE)

---

12. Each of Freddie's snakes measures 6 feet long. How much do 3 of his snakes measure together?

A. Not enough information
B. 18 feet
C. 9 feet

(ADVANCE 1 SPACE)

Problem Solving Speedway (Game Cards)

13. Mandy buys a basketball. She pays with a five-dollar bill and gets back $2.25 for change. How much did the basketball cost?

A. $3.75
B. $2.50
C. $2.75

(ADVANCE 2 SPACES)

14. Beth had 60 dog stickers, 55 cat stickers, and 23 fish stickers. How many stickers did she have in all?

A. 128
B. 148
C. 138

(ADVANCE 1 SPACE)

15. A new stereo costs $229 dollars. If Andrew had a $50-off coupon, how much will he need to buy the stereo?

A. $165
B. $179
C. $129

(ADVANCE 2 SPACES)

16. Steven wakes up at 6:30 A.M. to get ready for school. He is at school 45 minutes later. What time does Steven start school?

A. 7:35 A.M.
B. 7:45 A.M.
C. 7:15 A.M.

(ADVANCE 1 SPACE)

17. Sarah sang for 40 minutes and danced for 25 minutes one day. The next day, she danced for 35 minutes. How much time did she spend dancing on the two days?

A. 60 minutes
B. 100 minutes
C. 65 minutes

(ADVANCE 1 SPACE)

18. Ethan went to the store to buy 3 pencils for each of his friends. Ethan has 6 friends. Which shows how many pencils Ethan needs to buy?

A. 3 + 6
B. 6 + 6
C. 3 x 6

(ADVANCE 1 SPACE)

©Teacher Created Resources, Inc.

#8719 Standards-Based Activities & Games

Problem Solving Speedway (Game Cards)

#8719 Standards-Based Activities & Games

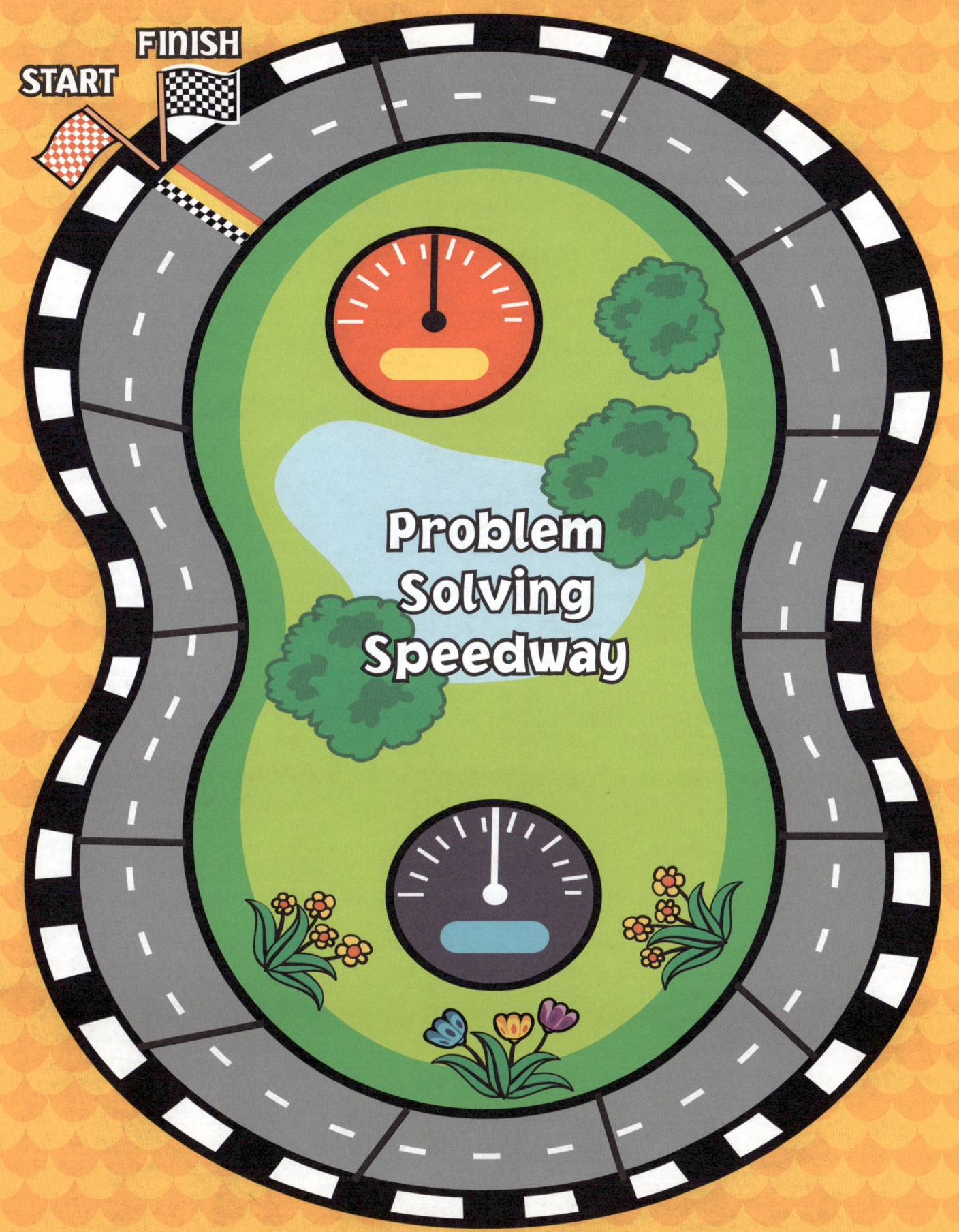

Problem Solving Speedway (Answer Key)

1. B
2. A
3. B
4. B
5. C
6. C
7. C
8. A
9. C
10. A
11. A
12. B
13. C
14. C
15. B
16. C
17. A
18. C

Game Markers

Subtraction Bowling

Skill: subtraction with or without regrouping

Standard: uses basic and advanced procedures while performing the processes of computation

Benchmark: performs basic mental computations

Materials

- a copy of Subtraction Bowling score sheet for each game played
- Subtraction Bowling game cards (red and green for no regrouping or blue and orange for regrouping)
- Subtraction Bowling game key
- paper and pencil

Suggested Use

- cooperative groups
- home connection
- tutorial
- centers

Directions (2 to 4 players)

1. Choose the green and red Subtraction Bowling game cards for no regrouping (or the blue and orange cards for regrouping). The cards are placed face up in draw piles according to color between the players.
2. Players write their names on the score sheet.
3. Player A draws a green Subtraction Bowling game card and a red Subtraction Bowling game card (or blue and orange). Using mental math or paper and pencil method, Player A subtracts the number on the red card <u>from</u> the number on the green card. The green card will always be the minuend (top number). If playing with the blue and orange cards, Player A subtracts the number on the orange card <u>from</u> the number on the blue card. The blue card will always be the minuend (top number).
4. Player A states the difference (answer) and uses the game key to find how many pins (points) to record on the score sheet. (*Note:* Players should check other players' answers before scoring.)
5. Player A returns the cards to the bottom of each draw pile.
6. It is then the next player's turn.
7. Game continues until each player has 10 turns. Each player totals his or her points on the score sheet. The player with the most points wins.

Reminder

If the digit in the subtrahend (bottom number) is larger than the minuend (top number) in the same place value, you must regroup.

Subtraction Bowling Score Sheet

Players' Names	1	2	3	4	5	6	7	8	9	10	TOTAL

Subtraction Bowling Score Sheet

Players' Names	1	2	3	4	5	6	7	8	9	10	TOTAL

Subtraction Bowling (No Regrouping Game Cards—green)

#8719 Standards-Based Activities & Games

Subtraction Bowling (No Regrouping Game Cards—red)

#8719 Standards-Based Activities & Games

Subtraction Bowling (Regrouping Game Cards—blue)

#8719 Standards-Based Activities & Games   152   ©Teacher Created Resources, Inc.

#8719 Standards-Based Activities & Games 154 ©Teacher Created Resources, Inc.

Subtraction Bowling Game Key

DIFFERENCE	NUMBER OF PINS
0–100	gutter ball = 0
101–200	1
201–300	2
301–400	3
401–500	4
501–600	5
601–700	6
701–800	7
801–900	8
901–1,000	9
over 1,000	Strike! = 10

- -

Subtraction Bowling Game Key

DIFFERENCE	NUMBER OF PINS
0–100	gutter ball = 0
101–200	1
201–300	2
301–400	3
401–500	4
501–600	5
601–700	6
701–800	7
801–900	8
901–1,000	9
over 1,000	Strike! = 10

#8719 Standards-Based Activities & Games 156 ©Teacher Created Resources, Inc.

The Terminator

Skill: math terms
Standard: uses basic and advanced procedures while performing the processes of computation
Benchmark: knows the language of basic operations

Materials
- The Terminator answer key
- The Terminator game cards
- The Terminator game board for each player
- game markers (chips, paper squares, etc.)
- The Terminator word bank (optional)

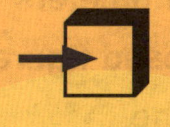

A flat surface of a figure.

Suggested Use
- cooperative groups
- tutorial
- home connection
- centers

Directions (2 players)

1. Each player receives a Terminator game board.
2. Terminator game cards are placed face down between players. (*Note to Teacher:* Use game cards relevant to current curriculum.)
3. Player A draws a game card and states the answer. (*Optional:* Use The Terminator Word Bank to help players.) Player B checks the answer on the answer key.
4. If a correct answer is given, the player places a game marker on the first letter (**T**) on The Terminator game board and the card is returned to the bottom of the draw pile.
5. If an incorrect answer is given, the player does not place a marker on a letter on The Terminator game board and the card is returned to the bottom of the draw pile.
6. If a "Terminator" card is drawn, the player covers the next letter. If an "Exterminator" card is drawn, the player loses a turn. The card is returned to the bottom of the draw pile.
7. Players continue drawing cards until one player has covered all the letters on The Terminator game board.

Reminder

Math terms are specific words used to describe math functions.

The Terminator (Answer Key)

1. quotient
2. line of symmetry
3. congruent
4. circle/pie
5. angle
6. area
7. capacity
8. centimeters
9. closed figure
10. cube
11. cylinder
12. data
13. decimal/decimal number
14. digits
15. elapsed time
16. equivalent
17. estimation
18. expanded notation/form
19. perimeter
20. yards
21. numerator
22. gallon
23. place value
24. line
25. bar
26. pound
27. pint
28. multiplicand
29. product
30. multiplier
31. difference
32. minuend
33. subtrahend
34. coordinates/coordinate pairs
35. commutative
36. acute
37. addends
38. sum
39. addition
40. A.M.
41. P.M.
42. array
43. fact family
44. face
45. certain
46. decimal point
47. denominator
48. numerator
49. divisor
50. dividend
51. quotient

The Terminator (Game Cards)

1.
$$5\overline{)175} \;\; \xrightarrow{} 35$$

2. This is the line that divides an object into two congruent parts.

3. Objects are _____ if they are the same size and shape.

4. This is a _____ graph.
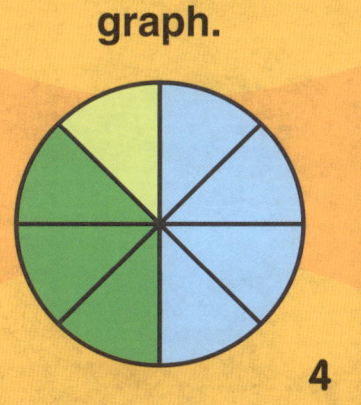

5. A figure where two lines meet at the same point is an _____.
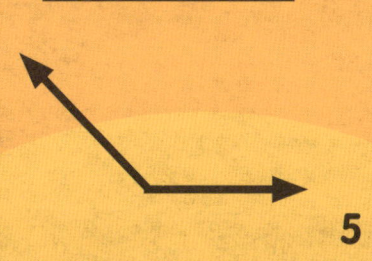

6. This is the number of square units covering the surface of a figure.

7. This is the quantity a container can hold when filled.

8. 100 _____ = 1 meter

9. A figure that starts and ends at the same point is a _____.

#8719 Standards-Based Activities & Games

The Terminator (Game Cards)

10. A solid figure with six square faces is a _____.

11. A solid figure shaped like a can is a _____.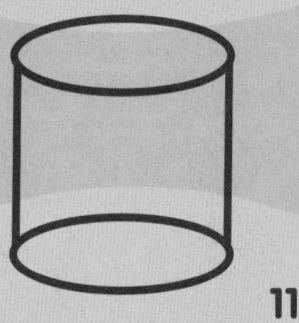

12. Collected information is called _____.

13. A number showing tenths, hundredths, etc. is called a _____.

.75

14. _____ are the 10 symbols used to write numbers.

1, 2, 3, 4, 5, etc.

15. _____ is the time between one activity and another.

16. Two or more sets that are the same amount are _____.

5 dimes = 50 cents

17. Rounding numbers to find out about how many is called _____.

18. This is a way of writing numbers showing place value.

300 + 40 + 2

#8719 Standards-Based Activities & Games

The Terminator (Game Cards)

19. The distance around a garden is called the _____.

20. This is the unit of measure used to measure the length of a football field.

21. In a fraction, the _____ tells the part of a whole.

→ $\dfrac{4}{5}$

22. Four quarts is the same as one _____.

23. The value of a numeral depending on its place in a number is called _____.

24.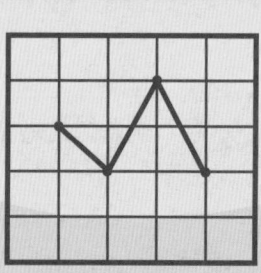
This is a _____ graph.

25.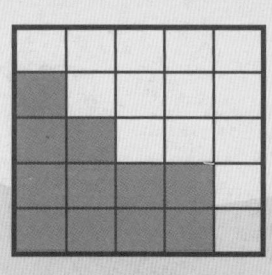
This is a _____ graph.

26. Sixteen ounces is the same as one _____.

27. Two cups is the same as one _____.

#8719 Standards-Based Activities & Games

The Terminator (Game Cards)

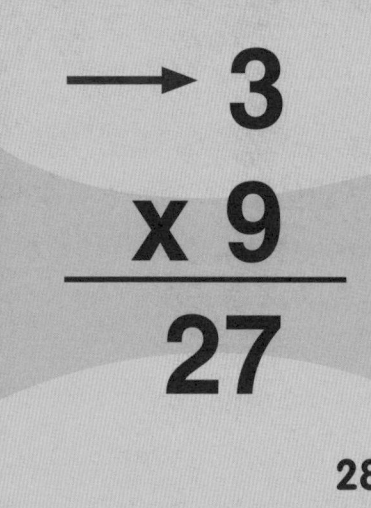

28

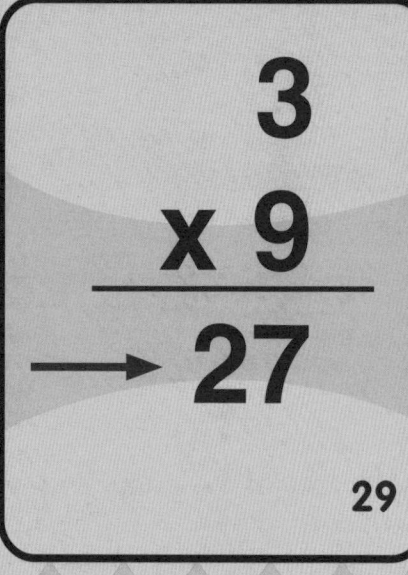

29

30

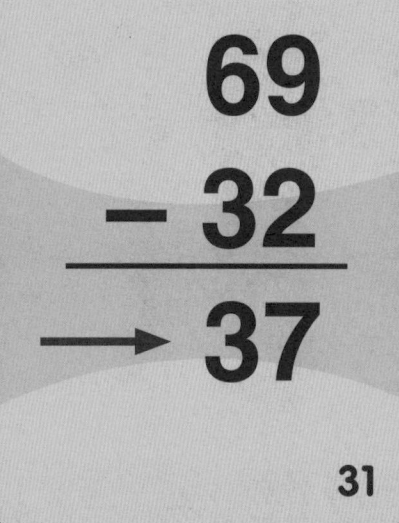

31

69
− 32
37

32

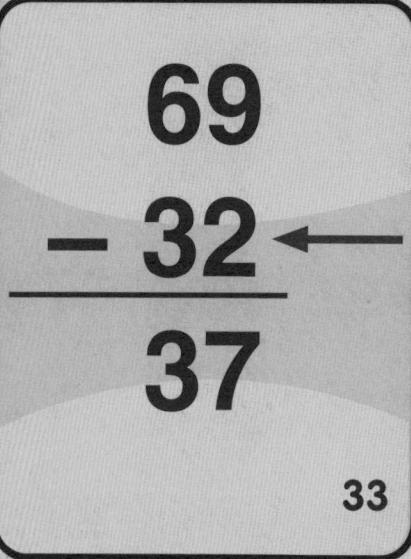

33

Pairs containing letters and numbers used to locate positions on grids are called _____.

(B, 3)

34

The _____ property of multiplication is when two numbers are multiplied in any order and the product is the same.

35

An angle that has a measure less than a 90° (right angle) is an

_____

angle.

36

©Teacher Created Resources, Inc. 165 #8719 Standards-Based Activities & Games

#8719 Standards-Based Activities & Games

The Terminator (Game Cards)

In the number sentence 8 + 4 = 12, the 8 and the 4 are called _____.

37

In the number sentence 8 + 4 = 12, the 12 is called the _____.

38

The opposite of subtraction is _____.

39

_____ is the time between midnight and noon.

40

_____ is the time between noon and midnight.

41

This is a display that shows objects in rows and columns.

xxxxxxxx

xxxxxxxx

xxxxxxxx

42

A set of related number sentences is called a _____.

3 x 4 = 12

4 x 3 = 12

12 ÷ 4 = 3

12 ÷ 3 = 4

43

A flat surface of a figure is called a _____.

44

In a probability experiment, if something is going to happen, it is _____.

45

#8719 Standards-Based Activities & Games

The Terminator (Game Cards)

The period that separates dollars from cents, or the whole number from the fractional part of a number, is called a _____. $35.98 45.6 **46**	This is the number in a fraction below the bar. $\dfrac{1}{\rightarrow 2}$ **47**	This is the number in a fraction above the bar. $\dfrac{\rightarrow 1}{2}$ **48**
 **49**	5⟌35 ↑ **50**	This is another name for the answer to a division problem. **51**
 Cover the Next Letter	 Cover the Next Letter	 Cover the Next Letter

#8719 Standards-Based Activities & Games

The Terminator (Game Cards/Extra Blank Cards)

#8719 Standards-Based Activities & Games

The Terminator (Game Boards)

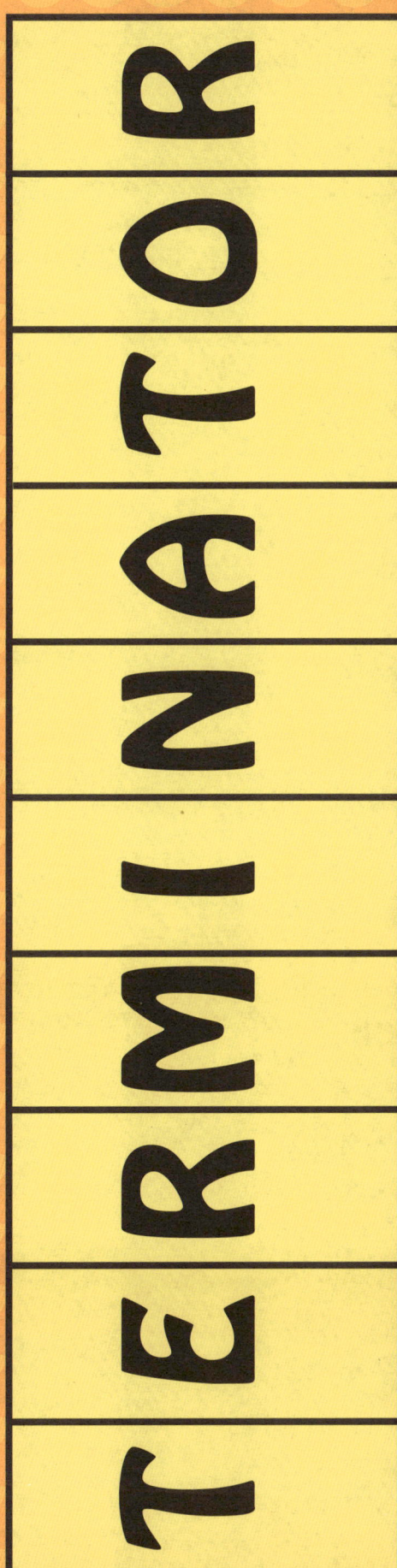
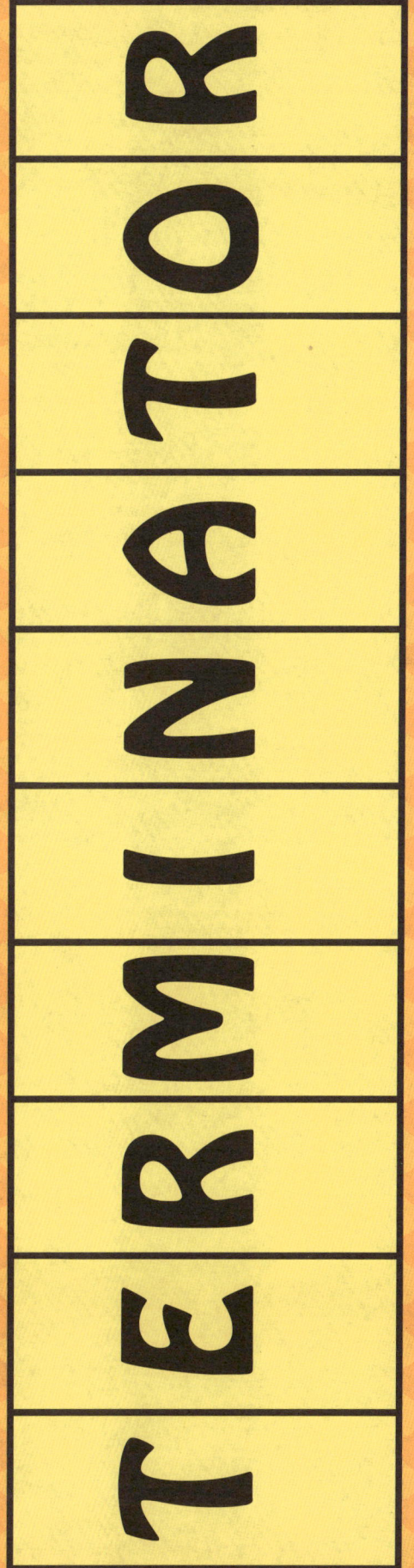

#8719 Standards-Based Activities & Games   174   ©Teacher Created Resources, Inc.

The Terminator (Word Bank)

A.M.	cylinder	line of symmetry
acute	data	minuend
addends	decimal/decimal number	multiplicand
addition	decimal point	multiplier
angle	denominator	numerator
area	difference	P.M.
array	digits	perimeter
bar	dividend	pint
capacity	divisor	place value
centimeters	elapsed time	pound
certain	equivalent	product
closed figure	estimation	quotient
circle/pie	expanded notation/form	subtrahend
commutative	face	sum
congruent	fact family	yards
coordinates	gallon	
cube	line	

#8719 Standards-Based Activities & Games